Park
Life

I would like to thank my family, especially my father, without whom this book would not have been possible.

I would also like to thank Nathan Jones for his Foreword, he is a true gentleman.

I would like to thank Jonny Gardner, Paul Hughes, Stuart and Phil Smith, Marc Rees and Andrew Dowling, also all of the boys at the Maindy Con Club, all of the boys at Ferndale Veterans football club, all of the boys at Ton Pentre Cricket Club, everyone at Ton and Gelli Boys' and Girls' Club and the fantastic team at Y Lolfa.

Finally thanks to anyone I have either played football with or against over the last 40 years. I literally enjoyed every minute of every game, thanks all.

Park Life

Four seasons of Rhondda football

Peter Roberts

First impression: 2019

© Copyright Peter Roberts & Y Lolfa Cyf., 2019

The contents of this book are subject to copyright, and may
not be reproduced by any means, mechanical or electronic,
without the prior, written consent of the publishers.

Cover design: Y Lolfa

ISBN: 978-1-78461-810-0

Published and printed in Wales
on paper from well-maintained forests by
Y Lolfa Cyf., Talybont, Ceredigion SY24 5HE
website www.ylolfa.com
e-mail ylolfa@ylolfa.com
tel 01970 832 304
fax 832 782

Foreword

I GREW UP in Blaenrhondda, a small picturesque village situated at the top of the Rhondda Valley.

At the heart of the village was Blaenrhondda Park an impressive football field at the foot of a vast mountain. An inspiring place to play football.

It was on Blaenrhondda Park representing Treherbert boys club at all age levels that my love affair with football began, and has continued ever since.

Where it all began, Blaenrhondda Park

It was also at this time I first came across Pete playing for Ton and Gelli Boys' Club.

We later went on to play on the same team for Treorchy Comprehensive School.

Since those times, I have found that the cut and thrust of football in the Rhondda gave me a good grounding for the ups and downs of my subsequent career, firstly as a professional player and now as a manager.

I enjoyed and valued my time playing football with Pete and many other good friends from the Rhondda and but for a few twists and turns here and there I might have even ended up in this book!

I am glad to read that grassroots football is alive and well and would like to wish Pete good luck with his book, I am sure all football fans will enjoy it as much as I did.

Diolch,

Nathan Jones

Manager, Stoke City Football Club

Contents

Rhondda Sporting Hall of Fame

THE RHONDDA VALLEYS (Fach and Fawr) are famous for coal mining. At one time there were over 70 pits within the two small valleys. Unfortunately, by the end of the 1980s there were no pits left in the Rhondda.

The coal mining industry created a strong social community, which expressed itself outside of the pit in male voice choirs, sport, politics, the pub and the workingman's club. Despite the mines (and their miners) now being a part of history, the strong community spirit they created lives on to this day.

As my account indicates this community spirit is evident and visible in grassroots sport in the area and although not many do (and nobody from the Maindy team) 'make it', many from the Rhondda Valleys have made it in their chosen sport. As you can see below it boasts a strong, proud sporting pedigree for such a small area:

Roy Paul born (1920) in Gelli – played football for Swansea City, Manchester City and Wales.
Famously captained Manchester City to an FA Cup win in

1956, and took the actual FA cup to local schools in the Rhondda.

The game is famous for Manchester City goalkeeper Bert Trautman playing on despite breaking his neck.

Cliff Morgan born (1930) in Trebanog – played rugby union for Cardiff, Wales and the British Lions.
Inaugural inductee of the International Rugby Hall of Fame
Captained Wales on the tour of South Africa in 1956, scoring a try in the 23-22 victory in the first test at Ellis Park in front of a crowd of more than 100,000.
Later became a BBC TV commentator.

Tommy Farr born (1913) in Clydach Vale – British Empire heavyweight boxing champion known as the 'Tonypandy Terror'.
Inducted into the Welsh Sports Hall of Fame in 1997.
In August 1937 Farr fought world heavyweight champion Joe Louis at the height of his career in New York City. He lost a split decision, a decision that was roundly booed by the 50,000 crowd.

John Bevan born (1950) in Tylorstown – played rugby union for Cardiff, Wales and the British Lions.
He also played rugby league for Warrington, Wales and Great Britain.
Played in the 1971 Wales rugby union Grand Slam winning team, scoring a try in the victory over England.

Jayne Ludlow born (1979) in Llwynynpia – played football for Milwall, Southhampton, Arsenal, New York and Wales.

Gained 69 caps for the Wales women's national team and is now the current Wales women's national team coach. Described as 'the best box-to-box player in the women's game', she scored 24 goals in the 2007 season helping Arsenal achieve the unprecedented quadruple.

Rob Page born (1974) in Llwynypia – played football for Watford, Sheffield United, Cardiff City, Coventry City, Huddersfield Town , Chesterfield and Wales.
Made over 450 league appearance and gained 41 caps for Wales.
Current manager of the Wales under 21 team.

Alan Curtis born (1954) in Pentre – played football for Swansea City, Leeds United, Southampton, Stoke City, Cardiff City and Wales.
Made more than 633 league appearances and gained 35 Wales caps.
Has been Swansea City caretaker manger on three separate occasions.

Nathan Jones born (1973) in Blaenrhondda – played football for Southend United, Brighton & Hove Albion, Scarborough and Yeovil Town.
Made over 450 league appearances.
Nathan has managed Brighton & Hove Albion, Luton Town and is current manager of Stoke City.

Mike Griffiths born (1962) Clydach Vale – played rugby union for Bridgend, Cardiff, Pontypridd, Wasps, Wales and the Barbarians.
Gained 35 caps for Wales.

James 'Jimmy' Murphy born (1910) Pentre – played
football for West Bromwich Albion, Swindon Town and
Wales.
Made over 200 league appearances and gained 15 caps
for Wales.
Managed the Wales national team in the 1958 World Cup
when they lost 1-0 to Brazil (the eventual winners) with
Pelé scoring the goal.
Manchester United assistant manager 1955 until 1971.
Blue plaque on his house in Treharne Street, Pentre.

Scott Young born (1976) Tonypandy, played football for
Cardiff City.
Made over 270 appearances for Cardiff City and also
managed the club on a caretaker basis.
Famously scored the winner in the 2002 FA cup giant
killing win over the then Premiership leaders Leeds
United.

Mal Evans born (1937) Gelli – Wales bowls champion.
Won the World Championship in 1972 and is still the
only Welshman to have held the men's singles title.

Griffith Morgan also known as Guto Nyth Bran born
(1700) Llwyncelyn – famous runner.
There is a statue of Guto Nyth Bran in Mountain Ash.
The Nos Galan race is an annual 5km race run on
New Year's Eve created as a memorial to Guto Nyth
Bran. Each year a mystery runner competes these have
included Iwan Thomas and Lynford Christie.

Clive Thomas born (1936) Treorchy – football referee.
Officiated at the 1974 and 1978 World Cups and also

1976 European Championships.
Infamously blew the whistle for full time as a corner kick
came into the box thus disallowing the late Zico goal
scored seconds later – which would have given Brazil a
2-1 win over Sweden in the 1978 World Cup.

Outside the world of sport, the Rhondda boasts many
other people who have made it in their chosen field, some
examples below:

Paul Whitehouse – comedian
Ian 'H' Watkins – pop star
Leanne Wood – politician
Annie Powell – politician
Donald Houston – actor
Glyn Houston – actor
Ron Berry – author
Rachel Trezise – author
Jill Evans – politician

I could go on, but you get the picture – the Rhondda
is punching above its weight contributing to the world of
sport and wider!

The Rhondda, a place I am proud to call home.

Introduction

THE GAME MAY still be 11 players versus 11, and the pitch is a similar size, but football has changed since the early games at the end of the nineteenth century.

The birth of the Premier League changed it. It is now big business – very big business. Who would have thought, back in 1961, when Jimmy Hill fought and overcame the salary cap (then £20 a week) that football players would be paid hundreds of thousands pounds a week? A week! Even a single game in the second tier of British football is reputedly worth a staggering £150 million to the winners, who get to grace the Premier League. A huge gulf exists between players and supporters; there is little or no common ground between them. The footballers themselves are now more likely to be from Portugal rather than Preston, Scandinavia rather than Scunthorpe, and the days are long gone when a Ford Cortina Mk 3 was the car that footballers dreamed of.

Supporters, on the other hand, who travel miles and pay good money attending games up and down the country, are only seen as customers. Customers, my arse!

During this period of change in the top echelons of football, luckily 'real football', as I call it, has not changed. Real football: where you have to pay contributions to play, hope that a referee turns up, get changed in a shed, play on a rain-sodden cabbage patch and even take your own kit home to wash. It is at this level of football, however, that a special camaraderie exists that is difficult to match elsewhere. Those of you who have played will know what I mean.

I have been involved in this real football for many years, as a player and as a manager, and what follows is an insight into four eventful seasons in a South Wales Sunday League. It is what amateur players and football fans can relate to, as the events like those detailed here happen every Saturday and Sundays up and down the country... providing there is a referee! As you will see, real football is truly a million miles away from the pampered prima donnas of the Premier League. It has provided me with the best of times.

A team is born

'I could have been a professional, you know!'

I WAS BORN in Neath, a typically rugby-mad town in the south-west of Wales. Despite this my love has always been for the round ball.

We moved to the village of Ton Pentre in the Rhondda Valley when I was four. I played my first game of 11-a-side football for Ton and Gelli Boys' Club under 10s team. I was seven, and can still vividly remember proudly putting the kit on for the very first time, soon followed by my brand new, sparkling football boots. I had even worn the boots to bed the night before. We lost 7-0 to the mighty Clydach Vale Boys' Club team, but I was hooked. Football mad after just one game.

Since then, apart from a brief interlude studying at and playing football for the University of Lampeter, I have played local grassroots football in the Rhondda Valley all of my life. Along the way, I have represented such stellar teams such as Ton and Gelli Boys' Club at all groups; Ton and Gelli Senior teams; Fagins; Maindy Con and Ferndale and District Veterans Team.

When I say played, I should say 'tried to play', as I could not (and still can't) do two of the game's basics: namely tackling, or heading the ball. Despite these footballing limitations, just like every amateur player I have ever met, after a few pints I will tell you quite convincingly that I could have been a professional before my injury. I'm sure that you have all heard these stories on countless occasions. You know the ones: 'I was going for trials at (insert club) before my injury (insert broken bone).'

My 'professional career-ending injury' was not some football-related leg break, the result of a last-ditch slide across the defender to score the winning goal in a cup final (I wish), but rather a broken leg sustained after grass sledging down a mountain straight into a fence. The sledging incident was not even in the snow, I should add! It took place in the middle of summer! The injury occurred when I was ten years old and robbed me of any pace I had, and the professional career I am sure would have followed.

In short, like thousands of amateur footballers up and down the country I am a limited footballer, but I absolutely love the game. My strength on the pitch, I have been told, is good close control. Good feet as they say in the game: absolutely essential if you are as slow as me.

Off the pitch I don't possess any great in-depth football knowledge. On the contrary, though I am a lifelong Cardiff City fan I have not gained much knowledge watching them. So I was not looking to become a manager when the opportunity to become player/manager of Maindy Con Football Club arose, especially as I still felt, despite my advancing years, that I had a lot to offer on the pitch. I did not even own a big, long, manager's coat with a difficult zip, nor had I had ever attended any media training sessions, but my love for the game ensured I agreed to take up the manager's role. The decision led to the following four eventful fun-filled seasons in the Sunday League.

The Maindy Conservative Club

Our name, Maindy Conservative Football Club, like the names of many other Sunday League teams, refers to the club where we were based socially.

Maindy Conservative Club

The club, known as the 'Con', is situated in a street of stereotypical terraced houses in Ton Pentre in the heart of the Rhondda Valley in South Wales. As the politically aware among you will note, a Conservative Club in the Rhondda Valley is an irony in itself. Suffice to say, there are no pictures of Winston Churchill or Margaret Thatcher on the walls. There are not even any Conservative voters that drink in the club... OK, there may be just one: Mr Marc Rees.

The Con is best described as old-fashioned, a throwback to bygone days. It is similar to many clubs in working class areas, struggling to make ends meet as the social media era takes over, the social media era that sees the younger generation of today glued to their iPhones or iPads, huddled in their bedrooms, rather than popping out to the club for a pint. Like pubs, these clubs are closing down at an alarming rate as a way of life is slowly being eroded. It is a great shame in my opinion.

Forgive my moaning about the youngsters of today. Back to describing the Con. Until recently, it enforced the following rules: no females allowed in the bar (apart from those serving, of course); no working clothes allowed in the snooker room. You get the picture!

Our football team was born when a small group of us who had been playing five-a-side together took the brave step and approached the powerful club committee to ask if they would help us run a football team. The support we requested involved them providing us with a kit, and paying the pitch fees to the local council. Pitch fees! I told you real football is a million miles from the Premiership.

We agreed to arrange everything else (somehow!) and counter-argued that we potentially could bring in extra custom on Sunday afternoons. We stressed that both teams would come back to the Con for refreshments after the game. This would coincide with the live Sky TV Super Sunday games and hopefully some would stay on for a drink, generating extra income. Our angle was that any extra custom for the club would be welcome. As these ideas often lead to nothing it was a gamble for the club's committee considering the tight financial constraints they were working within (thank the social media age again), but surprisingly they agreed to our request. 'Yes, boys,' said the treasurer. 'I think we can help you.' The then chairman, Mr Mike Eggert, was particularly supportive – so much so that he later became a valued Con player.

Living the dream

The dream was alive! Soon after, huddled around a table full of pints in the Con bar we agreed the administrative roles as follows: Jonny 'Gardner' Gardner became the football club chairman, Paul 'Hughesy' Hughes became the secretary and I became the treasurer.

Please, please, never underestimate these administrative roles in local football, or any amateur sport at any age level, for that matter. Without the dedicated servants that fill these positions there would simply be no games played each week. Never mind paying someone £200,000 per week to play, or the current government or FA directives on increasing participation in sport: without these unsung heroes there would be no amateur games taking place; then where would the next Gareth Bale or Paul Gascoigne emerge from?

It was at this point, that I was, somehow, also handed the management reins. Probably because nobody else would do it.

First managerial decision

My first managerial decision was to snap up Hughesy as my partner in crime; we became the management duo. Clough and Taylor we certainly were not; more like Cannon and Ball.

The Con Club committee were true to their word and provided us with a new kit, a very fetching green and white number. They must have had it cheap from somewhere (I'm not sure where) as I have never seen a kit quite like it before or since. I liked it, though, as it gave us our own identity.

Hughesy, in his new role as club secretary, then set about arranging our home pitch via the local council.

We ended up with the Astroturf in the nearby village of Pentre, not our first choice as we would have preferred a grass pitch. Astroturf sounds nice, but it was laid in the mid-1980s and is not quite like the nice third or fourth generation pitches you see nowadays. Think more like the QPR and Luton Town pitches of the mid-1980s, effectively a concrete block with lots of sand on it. You would certainly know about it for weeks if you made a sliding tackle as your legs would be cut and grazed for days after. Luckily tackling, let alone slide-tackling, was not part of my game. Others would be less fortunate; some of the boys still have the scars to prove it.

There were some murmurs of discontent from the boys with regard to playing on the 'Astro', as it is known locally, but considering the rain we have here in the Valleys I thought it was a good move. I also felt it might give us a footballing advantage, as the more you played on it the more familiar you became with the surface, much like QPR and Luton did in the 1980s. See – I was already thinking like a manager.

We then submitted a request to join the Rhondda Valley Sunday League, to Carol Hoskins, the legendary Rhondda League secretary. Carol has been the league secretary for as long as anyone in the Rhondda can remember, certainly since I was playing under 10s Boys' Club football. She is a perfect example of an unsung hero who has dedicated a lifetime to ensuring that football in the Rhondda Valley has thrived.

As I said, without these characters amateur sport would not happen.

We received the exciting news that our application was accepted. We were now a part of the Rhondda Valley Sunday League and were raring to go! The excitement increased further when we received the first month of fixtures. There were no full season fixtures at this level, but a set of fixtures for a month at a time.

Squad

We didn't have any foreign stars in our squad, not even anyone from Treherbert!

Our squad was made up of a group of boys from Ton Pentre. Many of us had known each other since school. Lots of us had received our football schooling at Ton and

Ton & Gelli Boys & Girls Club

Gelli Boys' Club, one of the oldest and proudest Boys' Clubs in Wales.

More recently, we had been playing five a side together on Sunday mornings. This is where the idea of forming an 11-a-side team was first mooted.

The squad included a variety of shapes, sizes, nicknames and football abilities. Some of the boys were playing regularly at a pretty decent standard on a Saturday, some had never played 11-a-side before and others, like me, were getting past their sell-by date. Like any other group of competitive young men it included a number of characters, including those who thought they were better than they were and others who thought they were the best, full stop. Not many fell into the category of lacking in confidence, but we were all good friends from the same town and hoping to have some fun on the football field in the all-star Rhondda Sunday League. Absolutely none of the squad was going to commit to the extent of foregoing their Saturday night drink for Sunday League football. Managing them would be fun!

Season 1

AFTER A COUPLE of hastily-arranged training sessions on the Astro and prior to the start of the actual season, we arranged a pre-season friendly to gauge our level. It was obviously not very good as we duly lost 9-3 to the Colliers, who, yep, you have guessed it, were based at a local pub of the same name. The Colliers were a team we would face later on in the league and one with whom we built up quite a rivalry.

Although we had been comprehensively beaten, we were still full of naïve confidence going into the league fixtures. Personally, all I can remember is my legs aching for days after the game and noting how many of the opposition had commented on our unusual green and white 'Pacers' kit. For those of you that were not around in the 1970s, two things stick out from that decade: Maggie Thatcher becoming Prime Minister, and Pacers, a popular distinctive green and white sweet. Our kit resembled the Pacers packaging.

First ever game

Our first-ever league fixture was away against Wattstown, a small town just over the mountain in the adjoining Rhondda Fach Valley, often referred to as the 'other Valley'. Nothing wrong with that, I hear you say, apart from the fact that we found out prior to the game that they had won the league for the previous two seasons, even going one season undefeated.

Great that we were playing 'The Invincibles' in our first game...

As if that was not bad enough most of our boys had been to a wedding the previous day and night and were visibly suffering from the excesses when we turned up. Hughesy, who had been best man at the wedding, was looking very pale indeed. He mentioned something about going in goal as we had been struggling for a goalkeeper, but unbeknown to him that problem had been resolved the previous day by local character Simon 'Scabby' Jones, who had agreed to help us out. I knew Simon was a footballer, but had never actually seen him play in goal and here we were about to start the season with him as our goalie. Gardner re-assured me: 'Pete, don't panic... Scabby will be great in goal!'

Luckily, unlike many other Sunday Leagues, kick off was at 2pm so those boys who were nursing hangovers had plenty of time to get some water on board. We arrived with 14 players, meaning luckily I did not have to dent anybody's pride by not including them in the first ever Maindy Con football squad. (This would not always be the case.) Diplomatically, I assured all 14 players present that they would be involved at some stage of the game. That included me.

Prior to kick-off, Jonny Gardner, who is the 'main man' in both the team and our group of friends in general, was chosen to wear the captain's armband. We did not have an actual armband – no way, that would have required too much forethought. He was our captain and our centre back, very much in the John Terry mould in that he loved a 50/50 challenge, but preferred them 40/60 against him.

The changing room was cramped and dark, but filled with excitement, anticipation and banter as we excitedly put on the green and white strip for our first league game. There was a determined scramble for the couple of pairs of large shorts. The smoke from Scabby's pre-match fag created a fog in the room as I scribbled down the names on the match card. I then left to give the referee the match card. On returning to the dressing room, the volume had gone up another level, but I could barely see a face, the cigarette smoke was that thick. I managed to get some quiet and announced the team through the smoke: 'The first ever Maindy Con starting line-up':

Goalkeeper: Simon 'Scabby' Jones (an excellent sportsman whose reactions had perhaps slowed up a little due to over-excess)

Left back: Paul 'Hughesy' Hughes (a solid left back; integral part of management team)

Centre back: John 'Evo' Evans (very good in the air, played lots of Saturday football and our most experienced player)

Centre back and captain: Jonny 'Gardner' Gardner (skipper/player who team bonded around, but with no real 11-a-side experience, loved a challenge and a big header)

Right back: Chris 'Evo' Evans: (a solid and very fit player but prone to the odd injury)

Centre midfield: Gary 'Gazza' Rees (an unknown quantity to me, as I had literally never seen him play before)

Centre midfield: Richard 'Tinker' Taylor (played regularly on a Saturday, very fit and skilful; predominantly left-footed)

Left wing: Stuart 'Smithy' Smith (a skilful winger with good balance; all left foot)

Right wing: Paul 'Brad' Green (very fit with a good engine and plenty of enthusiasm; dodgy shoulder, not able to take throw-ins)

Centre forward: Kris 'Geesy' Rees (skilful player with bags of energy and confidence in his own ability; also played regularly on a Saturday)

Centre forward: Steven 'Gabby, Jewell, etc etc' Davidson (I can't put all of Steven Davidson's nicknames down as it would be a very long book indeed; in fact, I could write a book just about Gabby. He is that sort of character. In brief, he thinks he is Pelé, but is actually more like Pavarotti. He is an excellent darts player though)

Along with our substitutes:

Pete 'Twinkle Toes' Roberts: preferably up front (decent feet/bad legs)

Robert 'Choc' Clarke: wide left (solid, very fit and the longest in the shower... by a mile)

Chris 'Moocha' Jones: anywhere (utility player, some may say a pound or two overweight)

Just before the leaving the changing room I said: 'We'll be playing 4-4-2 boys, I don't think that wing backs and hangovers go very well together.' They all seemed to agree.

As you can see from the photograph, we looked rather fetching in our green and white 'Pacers' kit. Back row (left to right): Stephen Davidson, Paul Green, Jon Gardner (skipper), Chris Evans, Stuart Smith, Gary Rees, Richard Taylor, John Evans. Front row: Simon Jones, Chris Jones, Kris Rees, Paul Hughes, Robert Clark, Peter Roberts (yours truly)

The game itself was a bit of a blur, especially as I had to go on early in the second half and add Jan-Molby-like size (and skills!) to the cause. It did not help, mind, as we were given a footballing lesson, eventually losing 3-0 to a team that included a number of players who were playing on a Saturday at a higher level, namely the Welsh League. This became a recurring theme coming across players who played at a higher level on a Saturday, who then joined their friends for a game on a Sunday.

After the game, as is customary in the Sunday League we went back to their club for refreshments – sandwiches and a few pints. Despite it being a Sunday afternoon their club was busy, with many people watching the Super

Sunday Premiership games on the big screen. Added to this, it is a well-known cultural fact that people in the Rhondda (or any South Wales valley for that matter) like a drink, as aptly described by the famous Valleys rockers the Manic Street Preachers: 'We don't talk about love, we only want to get drunk' (a line from one of their songs).

The after-match analysis continued back at the Con, and went on well into the evening, and generally we all seemed happy with our performance, despite the result. Much merriment surrounded our centre back Chris 'Evo' Evans' departure from the field after just 20 minutes with a bad back.

The evening ended late. I'm not sure how our girlfriends/wives felt about it, but I could sense this would become a regular Sunday evening event.

The following morning I went to work with a Monday morning hangover but pleased and relieved that we had played our first game and very much looking forward to the next weekend. The only shame was that there was a week of work in between.

First league point

We were away against the New Inn, who were based at a pub in Treherbert, a town at the very top of the Rhondda Fawr Valley – our valley. For those of you not familiar with the geography, it is so high that it has been known to snow there in August! There were no pre-match concerns about the New Inn as they were newcomers to the league, like ourselves, and therefore an unknown quantity.

Both teams battled hard in the first half, which ended goalless. Shortly into the second half two of our squad's characters, namely Gabby and Moucha, pestered me to put them on, so that they could change the game. I doubt that Pep Guardiola would have put up with this. Anyway, I gave in and put both of them on, but they didn't change the game. In fact, very unusually for Sunday League, the game ended goalless, although we could and should have won it in the very last minute when Chris Evans rose like a salmon at the far post, only to head over from less than a yard out. It would have been easier to score, honestly. Chris wears very thick glasses and was mercilessly reminded of this repeatedly in the changing room after the game. I think 'banter' is what they call it these days.

The game was also our first experience of a common 'real football' phenomenon, one which many of you who play will be aware of, namely the opposition 'linesman'. At this level the referee is in charge of the game very much on his own and therefore normal practice is to ask a representative from each team to run the lines: be the linesman in old money or the referee's assistant in new money.

I did our line to the best of my ability, giving everything as I saw it. However, the New Inn linesman (a very pleasant chap) gave us nothing all game. We were learning fast. Despite this it was our first-ever league point, a moment we were very proud of: 'the first point of many' was the general positive consensus after the game back in the Con.

Our first home game on the lovely Astro came next, against Trealaw. As it was our home ground, we had to pay for the referee (yes – pay for the referee!) prior to the game. It was hastily decided that if you started the game you paid £2 in contributions; substitutes were charged £1. The only exception to the rule was if you were not working at the time, you did not have to pay. It became my unenviable responsibility, as treasurer, to collect the coins from the boys and then pay the referee. I decided to try and collect the money before the game to pay the ref before the game, hoping that would give us some sort of edge with the referee. My older brother (a referee himself in the nearby Newport Gwent League) had advised me to do this, but it never seemed to work.

That first home game saw us score our first-ever goal. The honour and privilege of scoring it went to Chris Evans, a 20-yard strike into the top corner! He certainly enjoyed reliving the moment in the club after the game. By closing time Chris was telling everyone (who would listen) it was 'a 40-yard volley' into the top corner.

Unfortunately, however, the opposition had managed to score three.

Derby match

As with all football games against certain teams are more important than others, just ask any Cardiff City fan about the games against their fierce Welsh rivals Swansea City or a Rangers fan about their games against arch-enemies Celtic. Our next fixture, against local rivals Treorchy Prince of Wales, fell into this category.

Talking of football rivalries, my older brother, despite my allegiance to Cardiff City, was taken in by the Toshack years at Swansea and became a very rare bird indeed, a Rhondda Jack. As you can imagine, because of the well-documented animosity between sets of fans we were seldom able to watch the South Wales derby games together.

One memory of these games does stand out. We travelled together to an FA Cup first round game between the sides at Swansea in the early 1990s. The game was at the now long-forgotten Vetch Field, and we soon learned that travelling together was not a good idea. A minibus of us left early from the Rhondda, half full of Cardiff fans and half full of Swansea fans. The nearest safe place we could stop for a drink was a small town just outside Port Talbot, over 10 miles from Swansea! After a brief pint there we headed into Swansea and hit the traffic on the main road into Swansea, Fabian Way. As we did, hand-to-hand fighting was taking place either side of us in the middle of the road. The scenes were not uncommon in those days, but would be totally shocking today. We eventually made our way through the traffic (and fighting) and parked up in the Swansea Leisure Centre car park. There we all went our separate ways, some of the boys to the Cardiff away end and some heading to the infamous Swansea North Bank.

My mate Morris and I had not been able to get tickets for the away end, so we headed to the terracing beneath the big cantilever stand at the Vetch. We had previously decided this would be the best place to go. On our way to the ground we passed the Clarence pub, a Swansea stronghold. As we did, much to our displeasure and shock, we heard the words: 'Oi! You! Cardiff scum!' I turned around sharply to see who was shouting and to check if it was aimed at us. To my great surprise I saw one of the boys we had just got off the bus with! And it was indeed aimed at Chris and me. We made a very hasty getaway: getting caught out there was not advisable.

In the ground, mingling with the Jacks, we met two other Bluebirds who were studying at Swansea University at the time and very sensibly we all reminded each other we would have to keep a low profile. Morris failed this simple task as he leaped into the air arms aloft, following legend Nathan Blake's splendid goal for Cardiff. This resulted in a dig in the back for Morris and all of us constantly looking over our shoulders for the rest the game.

To make matters worse, Swansea went on to win the game 2-1, knocking Cardiff out of the cup. Morris and I had a very uncomfortable walk back to the Leisure Centre car park. Luckily, we made it out unscathed.

As I said our next fixture, against the Prince of Wales (Treorchy), also fell into this derby category and was eagerly awaited. We saw the Treorchy boys out the night before the game and much pre-match banter was exchanged. 'We're gonna smash you 6-0' in a drunken Valleys accent could be heard in popular local Ton Pentre hostelries such as the New Inn and Fagins.

The game itself was a tight affair, with much endeavour and enthusiasm from both teams but little in the way of skill; a typical Sunday League affair, which a journalist would describe as a bruising encounter. Stuart Smith tried his best to provide some flair, sticking to the left-hand touchline like glue and providing left-footed poise when given half the chance. Is it me or do all left-footed players look elegant when in full flow? The same can be said for left-handed cricketers: check out David Gower in his heyday. Elegant!

It was Stuart who won our decisive penalty kick, after being unceremoniously dumped to the ground as he was about to shoot.

As we had never had a penalty kick before and not having discussed who should take it if the situation arose, there was a moment of hesitation after the referee gave his decision. Everyone looked around thinking, who is going to take it? I did not need to get involved, mind, as Chris Evans confidently walked forward picking up the ball and declaring that he would take it. Just as confidently, he tucked the penalty past their keeper and into the bottom corner.

The result gave us our first-ever league win. '1-0 to the Maindy Con! 1-0 to the Maindy Con!' echoed loudly around the vibrant, post-match dressing room. Chris was quickly becoming our star player: still the only player to have ever scored for the Con.

Loads of the Treorchy boys came back to the Con after the game which helped to generate an excellent post-match atmosphere. Many good-natured pints were consumed while discussing and analysing the game. Unsurprisingly, the Treorchy boys were not happy with the penalty decision.

We had managed to arrange some after-match food, with each of us in the team (or, rather, our better halves) bringing something to add to the hastily-arranged food table we put together, which was laid out in the sacred club committee room. I took crisps, as they were easy. I can't see Mrs Pogba hand-making sandwiches and taking them to Old Trafford after the Manchester derby – can you? In line with true real football etiquette, the away team were invited to the food table first, followed by us. This was and still is the way.

The yard

The afternoon became even more memorable as it was the first appearance of the 'yard'. This was a three-pint cylinder that was normally safely hung up behind the bar in the Con, minding its own business. Not that day, though, as Chubby, the club steward, suggested each team have a whip-round and fill the yard and then present it to the man-of-the-match of each team. For fairness, they were given a choice of what to put in the yard: lager, cider, beer or even Guinness. It was then over to the man-of-the-match to do the tricky bit and drink it.

This soon became an entertaining regular post-match ritual along these lines: the man-of-the-match (or 'victim') would stand on a chair in the club lounge during half-time of the Sunday Sky game and attempt to drink the yard in front of everyone present. Even the boys from the snooker room would briefly put their cues down to come through to the lounge to have a look at the free entertainment. The ritual included much encouragement and vocal advice from the baying crowd (especially the women present), such as 'twist it' when the victim hit the bulb in the yard. Sound advice, I might add, as without a timely twist at the bulb stage the lager (or other drink of choice) would pour out onto the drinker, soaking them. If you don't believe me try it for yourself!

Other, simpler advice included 'drink the lot or show your cock' being excitedly sung and shouted as loud as possible. This was the normal routine unless Jonny 'Cast' was involved in the yard, when it would be as above but naked! If anyone was struggling to finish the yard, as many did, they would find a willing ally in 'Scabby' to help them. He just wanted the free booze to get drunk. In fact, Scabby would volunteer for a yard after every game, man-of-the-match or not!

I think the club committee realised they could be on to a winner after the Treorchy game. The takings must have rocketed. Fair play, they were a good bunch of boys. Added to this our partners, wives and girlfriends started coming to the club after the games, probably just to watch the yard being drunk.

Soon it became the norm for lots of us to stay, normally the same people, after the Sunday Sky game finished. The big screen would then display the music channels, creating a disco atmosphere. Our football team was helping to turn Sunday evening event into a wider event. Occasionally the music would be interrupted, if the wrong person got their hands on the Sky remote. A few seconds of the gentleman's entertainment channels would get an airing, before the music was hurriedly put back on.

Results improve

Our next fixture away at Pontygwaith saw a Con debut for recent signing Ian Lewis, a striker who, I had been told, had an eye for goal. Talking of his signing, there was no huge transfer fee, protracted agent led negotiations or even a bung involved. I didn't even promise him a birthday card like Yaha Touré would need. No, I simply bought Ian a pint, or knowing me, it was probably a Ken.

(Point of note: a Ken is half a pint, named after Ken Barlow who, the observant among you will know, only ever drinks halves on *Coronation Street*.)

Ian repaid his pint by scoring twice in a 4-0 victory that also saw skipper Jonny Gardner open his Con account with a typical brave header. Most surprisingly of all, our larger-than-life striker Steven 'Gabby' Davidson also opened his account and celebrated as if he had won the FA Cup. The sight of him running away to the corner flag, one arm aloft like Mr Shearer, only to realise that nobody was following him, was truly a sight to behold. It wasn't a bad finish though, fair play to him, calmly slotting home after rounding their keeper. I'm not sure that this result sent shock waves through the Rhondda Sunday League, but it certainly gave us some confidence.

We took the confidence forward winning our next game 10-3(!) against the Rhondda Hotel in Ferndale. Ian Lewis bagged six – what a signing, eh? This management lark is a doddle.

Chris Evans and Steven 'Gabby' Davidson each bagged a brace as well. Although this was an amazing result which we were rightly proud of against a strong Rhondda Hotel team, its importance dwindled later in the season when the Rhondda Hotel dropped out of the league and we lost the three points and the goal difference. I don't think that Jose Mourihno worries about beating West Ham or Everton and then finding out that all the hard work, effort and commitment has been undone because they have dropped out of the league. However, this is typical of most Sunday Leagues as participating in the league requires two things that most young men do not have: money and organisation. The contributions we collected covered paying the refs, but very unlike the professional game, the players themselves had to pay their own booking and/or sending-off fines. Getting sent off on a Sunday costs more than the team just going down to ten men.

Transfer market

After a couple of poor results that saw us lose against the Tynewedd Hotel and a strong Maerdy Social team, I stepped into the local transfer market again. This time I signed the brother of our midfielder Gary Rees, namely Leon Rees. He immediately helped us by scoring in a 4-3 win over Blaenllechau (try saying that after a couple of pints). Ian Lewis also scored. More surprisingly, though, club veteran (even older than me) Marc 'Bealo' Rees opened his account for the Con. 'A Conservative scoring for the Conservatives!' was how he excitedly described it in the club that night.

At this point in the season, scoring goals was not a problem. We were a bit like Newcastle under Kevin Keegan, confident we would score more goals than the opposition. It was a bit of a surprise when we failed to score in our next game, losing 4-0 to the Railway Inn. They were a very strong, established team though.

We got back to scoring ways and extracted our revenge on the Colliers for our pre-season friendly defeat by beating them 3-1.

The imaginatively named Rhondda League Cup came next, but we didn't last long, losing 4-1 in the first round against the New Inn.

Our final game before the 'Christmas break' was a 1-1 draw against the Tynewydd Hotel. When I say the Christmas break, I am not making reference to the Rhondda League having an innovative winter break strategically set up to let players recuperate. No, it is an annual informal winter break when the weather gets so bad and the pitches so poor that most of the games in December and January are called off because of waterlogged pitches. This is where our Astro turf pitch helped, however, as we were able to play just after the New Year, beating Pontygwaith and the Boar's Head.

No ref – over to you gaffer

Our next fixture away to Blaenllechau would normally have been uneventful, except that when we arrived there was not a referee. This was very frustrating; the lack of a ref is a real disappointment, especially when the two teams are present and ready to go. However, it does happen as just like in any local league there is a lack of referees. The game can then be cancelled, or the teams can agree to play it with a 'ref' from either team. Sometimes a decision is even taken that a representative from each team referees one half each – for fairness sake! None of these outcomes are particularly satisfactory and I can't see Mourinho agreeing with it, but they do ensure that a game can be played.

On this occasion the unenviable task of refereeing the game went to yours truly. I should have known better as my brother had repeatedly told me vivid stories of how much hassle being a local football referee is. (I'm sure he could write a book about refereeing tales himself if he could get off his lazy arse.) Making matters worse, I was there representing one of the teams involved, so I was on a hiding to nothing as I blew the whistle to start the game. It did mean I earned a couple of quid, though. Every cloud has a silver lining.

Luckily there were no real flare-ups in a game we won 3-1, courtesy of a splendid Leon Rees hat-trick but I did go to bed that night with the words: 'C'mon, ref, you prick!' ringing in my ears, most of the abuse having come from my own players.

The experience of refereeing the game was a real eye-opener for me and it certainly made me consider my reaction to referee decisions in the future. Having done it, I would suggest that managers at all levels of the game referee a game and then perhaps they would be less likely to blame them for their teams' failures. It makes me wonder how Neil Warnock is a qualified referee but still gives out so much shit! I'm not sure if Wenger would be any good, mind, as all he would do is say 'I didn't see that incident' in a French accent.

Our next fixture was against a strong Railway Inn side, in a game that was personally memorable for me as I notched my first goal for the Con. Despite this personal highlight, we lost the game 6-2. After analysing, and re-analysing, my goal (a tap-in from all of a yard out following a goal line melée), which got better with every pint back at the club, it was time to go home, albeit with the old wobbly wellies on. Another slow Monday in work beckoned.

Following my first goal, I was full of confidence as I came off the bench against the Colliers and managed to notch again in an exciting 3-3 draw. Two goals in two games, all together now… 'The player/manager's on fire – your defence is terrified!' We would have won as well if Ian Lewis had scored a late penalty, but the ball went high over the bar and I believe it's still travelling! Weirdly, Ian blamed it on the ball being too soft.

The final few games of the season saw us lose to Maerdy Social, lose to Trealaw and beat the Boar's Head. The game against the Boar's Head saw Stuart Smith score his first goal for the Con, having been an ever-present in the side throughout the season. Obviously the goal was scored with his left foot.

Before our last fixture of the season we were very disappointed to learn that Pontygwaith had also dropped out of the league, meaning we lost six points and a couple of league places as a result.

The last game of the season was away to local rivals Treorchy. It was another hard-fought close game. This time, however, they managed to win the game 2-1, extracting their revenge for us winning the home game earlier in the season.

Oldest player in the league

The game saw a Con debut for Phil Smith, father of Con regular Stuart Smith and, without wanting to upset him, probably the oldest player ever to have played in the Rhondda Sunday League – or any league, for that matter. He lasted 25 minutes, hugging the left-hand touchline (now we could see where Stuart got it from), and we all enjoyed it immensely when he dummied, stepped inside and skinned two boys who were at least half his age. I'm sure he enjoyed it as he was grinning from ear to ear when he came off to rapturous applause from our boys.

We might have lost the game, but we definitely gave as good as we got in the drinking games back at their pub, the Prince of Wales. We were all suitably tipsy and up for it when Gardner suggested a pub crawl back from the Prince to the Con. Everyone was in drunken agreement.

The crawl saw us visit exciting establishments such as the Griffin Inn and the Pentre Legion Club. We were not a pretty sight when we got back to the Con, and it was certainly not the right time for the yard to rear its ugly head. Obviously I had not had a yard during the season as it required the pre-requisite of winning man-of-the-match, but the boys took it upon themselves to start throwing money into a pint pot and awarding yards for absolutely anything... Discussions led to yards being bought for a variety of quickly-decided 'awards' including best goal, best foul, best dive... anything really! The yards were being readily handed out.

It wasn't long before Gardner suggested it would be

a good idea to get one for the player/manager and before I could say anything in my defence it was there, frothing and glistening in front of my already drunken eyes. I was not confident as I took my position on the yard chair, and less so once the advice started:

'Twist it, Roberts, twist it.'

'Drink the lot or show your cock!'

As I'd already 'had a few', as they say in these parts, I forgot to twist the yard at the crucial bulb stage, which meant a very wet T-shirt, but thankfully not quite so much lager. This sounds like a clever ploy but I was too drunk for that: I just simply forgot to twist the yard. Whatever, I certainly don't remember much after drinking the yard, apart from my much better half Michelle having to come down to the club to collect me and take me home. How embarrassing.

On reflection, it was a successful first season in that we won a few games, lost a few, but more significantly managed to complete all our fixtures without dropping out of the league. No mean feat. We had also had a great laugh along the way.

The Con Club itself was very happy with the popularity of the club following our games. This success meant that the club committee agreed to sponsor us for the following season.

Presentation night

All that was left for us to do was to celebrate at our end of season presentation night. We decided to use the function room upstairs in the club. I spent the days before preparing a summary of the season.

Not being sure how it would go down I was a bit

nervous as I took the mic, summarising the season game by game, goal by goal, incident by incident. I admit it did go on a bit but everyone seemed to enjoy it as the lager and beer flowed freely. Following my season review, Hughesy then acted as my pretty assistant and gave out the end-of-season awards. They were won as follows:

Maindy Con FC player awards – Season 1:

> Players' Player: Jon Gardner
>
> Player of the Year, achieved for most man-of-the-match awards: Kris 'Geesy' Rees
>
> Most Improved Player: Paul 'Brad' Green
>
> Clubman of the Year: Rob 'Choc' Clarke
>
> Top Goal Scorer: Kris 'Geesy' Rees

We had the trophies engraved at a cobblers/engravers in Treorchy, where the gentleman could swear more than any other person I have ever met. Despite his language, I must say he made a great job of the trophies.

I couldn't say the same thing about the local disco that we had booked. They played none of the music any of us liked and did not have, or would not play, any of the music we asked for. Thinking of the fact that the disco had cost us over £70 to book, and being a frugal so-and-so (a right tight bastard), I said to Hughesy: 'Next year we'll do our own disco'. And so the Con management team became the club DJ-ing duo as well. Watch out Judge Jules! (Not likely, we looked more like Smashie and Nicey.)

Season 2

BEFORE THE START of the second season our squad was weakened, as we lost influential midfield man Leon Rees. Losing him was bad enough; finding out he'd signed for local rivals the Railway Inn was even worse.

Following the loss of Leon, I entered the local 'transfer market', signing three youngsters, namely Matthew Pugh, James Chick and Lewis Thomas. They were friends who regularly came to the club and we signed them as a group. They were more commonly known as the 'three ills' due to their bad behaviour after a couple of pints, so I thought they would fit right into our squad. Following their signings, I felt our squad was stronger than last season; added to that we had a season's league experience under our belt. We should be able to give any team a good game, I thought.

The season kicked off with a home fixture against a new team to the league, the Max Club from Clydach Vale, which we won 9-4 including a brace of goals coming from the late sub, yours truly. I won't bore you with the details but one was a powder puff shot from outside the box that their keeper very kindly dived over the top of. I was, very briefly, joint top scorer, along with Gary Rees, Gabby and Kris 'Geesy' Rees, who all also notched two goals each. The game, however, was marred by some eccentric refereeing by the local 'Clive Thomas' impersonator, Stuart Jones.

We were to see Mr Jones again later in the season. On this occasion, however, he worked in our favour by correctly sending off one of the Max Club team early on, thus contributing to our 9-4 victory. His performance did not impress the Max management team, though, who gave him a big zero out of ten on the official match referee card. I have never seen this before or since and it would surely have resulted in a large fine for the Max Club, had they not dropped out of the league soon after this, their one and only fixture. Three points gone and top of the table position gone in a flash. I did decide to allow the goals scored to count in the end-of-season tally. (A decision that had nothing to do with my two goals, I might add.)

Our next game was a tough assignment away at Mount Pleasant, made even trickier by a long injury list including skipper Jonny Gardner. It meant that two of the three younger members of the squad, namely James 'Chicky' Chick and Matthew 'Pughy' Pugh, made their debuts. Chicky capped his debut with a man-of-the-match performance in a 4-1 defeat.

Wins against the Pentre Legion and Blaenllechau followed.

The game against Blaenllechau saw us give a debut to local legend Lee Tapper who was playing for Ton Pentre, champions of the Welsh League Division 1 at the time. After the game, he endured an evening of 'Lee, Lee, Lee Tapper' being drunkenly bawled out at him repeatedly in the club. It must have impressed him, as he never played for us again.

The lack of a referee threatened to affect our next game against the Colliers, but luckily centre back John Evans agreed to be shouted at this time – in other words, be the referee. I had learned my lesson after the last time. Perhaps John was thinking of the money?

Too many players

Despite John offering to ref, we still had 21 fit and willing players turn up, which gave Hughesy and me a management selection headache. We could only name 16 players, and even then two would get changed for no reason as you could only use three subs.

Some of the boys like Jonny Cast and Brad made it easy for us by offering to sit the game out. This was very decent of them as it made the job of picking the squad that much easier. Considering how hard this was, I am a strong advocate of being able to use more than three subs in local football if a team has them available. In fact, I think that all the teams in local leagues should agree at the start of the season that if a team has four, five, or even six subs, then if they want to, they can use them. Otherwise boys are turning up and foregoing their Saturday afternoon or Sunday afternoon for no reason. This is a real shame, which does absolutely nothing to encourage and increase participation in the beautiful game.

John had an easy ride as ref. We won a one-sided game 11-1, with a fine, sublime performance from man-of-the-match Geesy. It wasn't until after the game that it became apparent to me that Geesy had been in a boozy altercation with a number of their team the night before. They had repeatedly questioned his football ability (among other things) and hence his wonderful performance during the game.

Abandoned game

The 11-1 victory set us up nicely for our next game, away at the Railway Inn in the first round of the Rhondda Cup.

The Railway were a strong, experienced team who had beaten us convincingly twice last season. I was expecting a difficult game, especially as it was at their place. Their pitch is renowned locally for two things: one, it's a long walk from the changing rooms, which are attached to the local sports centre; and two: the shovel.

This shovel, left strategically at the side of the pitch, was to be used as and when required to pick up the dog shit on the field. Unfortunately the shovel was frequently required, as dog shit is a common disgusting problem on pitches that are not fenced off. (Once again, this is not a problem our friends in the Premier League have to concern themselves with.) There have been some terrible incidents with people getting infected from dog shit on the pitch. Surely the council could fence the pitches off?

Nobody wanted to take responsibility for the shovel. It was not a pleasant job, but a necessary evil. Never mind the pitch or the shovel, the game itself turned out to be memorable for all the wrong reasons, and was so bizarre it is probably not even typical in the crazy world of real football. You make your own mind up!

It started badly when our goalkeeper Scabby went to the wrong pitch. I put it down to a breakdown in communication, rather than how much Scabby had refuelled the evening before. Chris Evans drew the short straw and agreed to go in goal. I was quite confident with 'Evo' grabbing the gloves. I had seen him play there before and he had made a decent job of it. My confidence was misguided. After only a couple of minutes he somehow managed to dive over the top of a back pass-type shot that trickled into the corner of the net. To make matters worse their goal was scored by ex-Maindy Con man Leon Rees.

Leon certainly enjoyed it as he ran past 'our touchline' to celebrate.

We did not drop our heads, however, but rather regrouped and started to boss the game. We were deservedly 3-1 up at half time, following excellent goals from Geesy, Ian Lewis and Gary Rees (Leon's brother). I could see that their experienced manager Nigel was worried at the break. I gave an intelligent half time talk: 'Boys, if we shut them out at the back, then we've won'.

However, I had a feeling we would struggle in the second half as most of the boys had been to Cardiff the night before for a big swig. On returning, they had ended up back at skipper Gardner's house, where the drinking continued until the early hours of the morning. It was rumoured that some of the boys were wandering the streets of Ton Pentre at 5am, and for some strange reason they were wearing the club kit.

It was no surprise to me, then, when Chicky asked to come off at half time, as he was suffering from the previous night's excesses. I replaced him with our super sub Breezy. (Our very own David Fairclough.) In all honesty, I was expecting a few more to come off as the previous night took its toll.

What I wasn't expecting was for Gary Rees to foul (a diplomatic description of the tackle) an opponent and get a deserved red card. Unfortunately for Gary he broke his own nose in the process and went straight off to hospital. As a result we were down to 10 men and soon had to make further substitutions (Choc and myself both going on) as the previous night caught up with a couple of the boys. With our numerical disadvantage, it was no surprise when they got a goal back; our chances of holding on for an unlikely victory were dealt a further blow when super-sub Breezy went off injured. We were down to nine men.

Despite a gallant effort by the nine of us, the Railway eventually equalised with four minutes remaining and at the final whistle it finished 3-3. The boys were gutted, as with the numbers as they were it was inevitable that we would lose in extra time. And so it transpired as the Railway scored four goals in the first half of extra time, and we were effectively out of the cup at 7-3 down. During the second half of extra time, to add injury to imminent defeat, Geesy went off hurt and we were down to eight players. Predictably, the Railway dominated the remainder of game and scored another two goals and that should have been that.

But no, our friend Stuart 'Clive Thomas' Jones decided to make a name for himself (albeit in very local circles) by sending off Hughesy for a deliberate handball with only a couple of minutes remaining. It was a very harsh decision and even more bizarre considering the game was not in the balance. But Stuart, lacking common sense in our opinion, insisted, and Hughesy received his marching orders. As he was trudging off, it all became too much for skipper Gardner, who lost his cool and the red mist descended. He sent the ref Stuart a verbal volley with most of the words ending in 'off'. Stuart, again not using common sense, but in this case adhering to the letter of the law, then sent Gardner off for foul and abusive language.

Ugly scenes followed as Gardner continued the expletives as he slowly left the field, while Stuart further inflamed the situation stating to Jonny that he would write a white paper – a written report to the Association. Gardner's final word as he left the field – 'Send a white paper in and I'll wipe my arse with it' – are now legendary in the Maindy Con and are often quoted as the pints are consumed and games recalled.

When it eventually all calmed down, and with Stuart about to restart the game, he suddenly realised that we only had six players left on the field and promptly abandoned the game.

The result stood, however, and we were out of the cup. That score of 3-1 up at the break seemed an awful long time away as we made the long walk from the Railway's pitch to the changing rooms in the sports centre. To be honest I don't even think the Railway players could believe the outcome, but they didn't sound too bothered as they celebrated in the next changing room. At least Nigel had the good grace to tell me that Stuart could have avoided the last two red cards. Implications followed the game, resulting in Hughesy, as our secretary, having to write to the Rhondda League and the South Wales Football Association to apologise on our behalf and explain the situation from our point of view.

The final outcome was that we got fined as a club and the three sent-off players (Gary Rees, Hughesy and captain Jon Gardner) were all fined individually and banned for various numbers of games. It was a low point in the season, which could have finished us as a club with the fines the team incurred and the individual fines the boys got. However, we eventually moved on and I comforted myself by saying that it was only the cup and we were never going to win one of them. After the abandoned game things became quite difficult and there was some bad feeling in our dressing room for the first time.

This was quite prominent following a 7-1 loss to Trealaw.

Unrest/management duo resign

In the lounge of the Con after the game, there were even calls for the management team to step down, albeit the loudest calls were coming from Gabby, so nobody really listened.

Normality was restored against local rivals Treorchy, with a 4-1 win in a game that started in lovely weather and ended up in torrential sideways hailstones. It was like having four seasons in a day, typical Welsh weather! The weather got so bad towards the end of the game there was even a rumour that Jonny Cast (a very gifted musician and enthusiastic footballer) nearly scored, but no one could confirm or deny this. They did not see his effort as it was directly into the hailstones. He still maintains to this day that it was very close.

The win calmed the calls for the management duo to be replaced, and Jonny Cast helped the feelgood factor return by celebrating his near goal with a naked yard in the club.

He followed this up with a drunken bet with all the boys present (about nine of us) that for a pound from each of us he would eat the inside of one of the air fresheners from the lounge. (Please bear in mind that these air fresheners had been in the club for at least 10 years, sitting on the not too clean windowsills.)

We watched in disbelief as Jonny opened the air freshener, removed the jelly-like substance inside (which was now hard and crusted) and promptly ate all of it... in one go. He gained £9 for this. Pure madness.

The goalposts are stolen

Our next game was cancelled. Not because of any normal reason like bad weather or no ref being available. No, this time it was a new reason. Both teams were present when I arrived and I found it quite odd that the boys were saying to me, 'Pete, looks like the game is off.' I assumed the ref had not turned up and that we could hopefully arrange something between ourselves, but no: on speaking to the 'Parkie' it transpired that the two top horizontal goal posts had been stolen overnight.

'They were here when I left after yesterday's game... someone must have pinched them last night,' he said.

Who would want to steal them? I thought (and still think) to myself. That was that though, and the game was cancelled by the ref. The game was in Treherbert, mind, which might explain the theft (apologies to any readers from Treherbert).

The Railway Inn again

Our next game was against the Railway and was severely disrupted as it clashed with centre back Brad's stag weekend up in sunny Scotland. This meant we were missing 10 regular players who had very wisely decided that a piss-up in Scotland would be a better laugh than losing to the Railway again. Despite this, and illustrating our squad strength in numbers, we managed to field a team, albeit a weakened one. The team included the dream striking partnership team of myself and Gabby. One thing for sure was that the Railway would not require much pace at the back. Having never beaten the Railway, with missing players, and with the recent abandoned game fresh in the memory, we weren't expecting much. Despite this we managed two wonder goals, one from youngster Lewis Thomas, who literally beat eight Railway players before calmly side-footing an assured finish into the net, and a great volley from Geesy. The score was 2-2 with minutes left. Then disaster struck and they scored the winner in the last minute. Cue major celebrations on their behalf. The result was relayed to the boys up in Scotland, but I am assured they still managed to enjoy themselves despite the result. It was a great performance considering the circumstances, but the Railway were definitely becoming our bogey team.

Two further defeats followed this game, including an embarrassing 6-2 reverse away to 10-man Blaenllechau.

South Wales Intermediate Cup

Our next game came as a bit of a shock for me, as Hughesy had entered us into the South Wales Intermediate Sunday Cup. It was a competition open to all of the Sunday League teams in South Wales. I had never heard of it. Apparently we had not been eligible to enter before, as the rules stated you had to have existed as a club for more than one season to enter. But Hughesy, a proactive secretary, had entered us for this year.

We were drawn at home against Penybont Rangers of the nearby Bridgend League. It was a second-round game, as we had received a bye in the first round due to odd numbers of teams that had entered. Despite struggling with the bans from the recently abandoned game, we managed to put out a very competitive team. It was a very cold day and turned out to be a close game against a good competitive Penybont Rangers side. With minutes remaining it was 1-1, when Tinker broke into the box and squared it across the goal to find young Matthew Pugh at the far post, who managed to steer it home from all of a yard out. He then went off on a mad celebration towards the corner flag, which we all joined in with.

The rumour back in the club after the match was that Penybont let us win because they did not want to be in the darkest deepest Rhondda for extra time, although I didn't believe it for a minute. After a few post-match celebratory pints in the club, Pughy gleefully told us all he had actually hit it in with his cock. 'Scores with his cock, he even scores with his cock' was soon being bellowed out by the boys!

'Never mind,' I told him, 'they all count, and it was the bloody winner!' I thought our victory was more down to them not being accustomed to our Astro pitch, but the game will always be remembered for Matthew Pugh's 'cock winner'.

Following the game, discussions turned to who we might get in the next round – the quarter-final!

Same team twice in a row

Playing the same team twice in two weeks in any league is never easy, but in the Sunday League it can create many problems: fouls are remembered and grudges kept. The quirk of the fixtures meant that this occurred in our next set of fixtures as we played against the Rhondda Hotel, Porth, two Sundays in a row. And to illustrate the inconsistencies of football at this level, we lost 7-4 away and then won the home game 7-1.

I missed the second game as I was at the hospital for the birth of my daughter. (I know shocking ... I should have been at the football). But it was memorable for a super hat-trick by Stuart Smith, proving he is a chip off the old block. Hughesy was also absent, which meant a temporary management team of Brad and Evo in charge for the first time… one game, one win; they began referring to themselves as the management dream team.

After the weather-enforced Christmas break we drew 2-2 with the Pentre Labour Club, a poor result in a game memorable for Hughesy, as he went in goal after Scabby was sent off.

This was followed by a 5-1 win over Mount Pleasant in a game that saw a debut in goals for Lee Scott and the start of a passing of the guard in relation to the goalkeeper position, as Lee slowly began to take over from Scabby.

Transfer news

The big news after this game was the shock transfer of Gabby to local rivals the Colliers. I assumed the Colliers knew what they were letting themselves in for!

South Wales Intermediate Cup – quarter-final

Everyone was up for the next game, the quarter-final of the SW Intermediate Cup. We had been drawn at home, this time against fellow Rhondda League team Trealaw. Although everyone was upbeat, personally I didn't hold out much hope, as they were the current Rhondda League champions and had recently beaten us in the league. I was really pleased to have the game at home, mind, and was hoping that we would be able to put out our strongest team to be competitive.

There was a difficult managerial decision before the game between either Scabby or Lee Scott in goal. After much deliberation, Hughesy and I decided to stick with Scabby, the main reason being that he had never let us down before. The game went exactly to plan with Geesy and Tinker at the forefront both scoring a goal each and helping us win 2-0.

The crowd that came to see us (approximately 50!) were also a great help. I don't know who was more shocked after the game, them for losing or us for winning. All I could think was if we won the next game we would have a final to look forward to.

A very drunken evening followed down at the Hibernia Club in Gelli (for a change) with club veteran Bealo getting carried away and staying out a little longer than he had planned. This resulted in him returning home to find that his better half had put his dinner in the bin. Better get in on time next time, Mr Rees!

We lost our next two league games against the Railway Inn again (3-1) and Maerdy Social (4-0). Unfortunately we also lost Bealo to an ankle ligament injury, which was not good news with the semi-final of the Intermediate Cup coming up.

South Wales Intermediate Cup – semi-final

Very luckily we were drawn at home (again) in the semi-final, but less fortunately our opponents were fellow Rhondda League team Maerdy Social. They had not only just beaten us 4-0 in the league, but were a team we had never taken any points from, so we were really up against it. I was just pleased to have a home draw, to use the advantage of the Astro pitch. Our preparation for the game was marred by a long injury list, which added to Maerdy's overflowing confidence when they arrived.

I don't know why but I could sense a cup shock was on the cards, maybe because they were so confident. And so it transpired as we managed to upset the odds, producing a massive cup shock by winning the game 2-0. Our goals were courtesy of a splendid 25-yard volley into the top bin by Geesy and another nice and tidy finish from Ian Lewis. Everybody played really well.

The above article appeared in our esteemed local newspaper, the *Rhondda Leader!*

Afterwards the Maerdy boys did not come back to the club for the customary pint and food, meaning all the food we put on was for us. We then headed off for another drunken night down the Hibs.

Hughesy and I then set about making the arrangements and logistical preparations for the final, which included trying to find out where the final would be played. (Not a problem that Premiership managers or stars would have to contend with.) We made numerous phone calls to the league secretary (the institution that is Carol Hoskins), resulting in our hopes being raised that the final would be played at Penydarren Park, home of Merthyr Tydfil Football Club.

Now that really would have been something.

Unfortunately, this did not happen. The final was eventually arranged to take place at Maesteg Park FC. This decision was made because it was located centrally between us and the other finalists, namely Cwmafan Phoenix of the Neath and Port Talbot League. Hughesy then set about arranging a 52-seater bus from the Con Club, remembering that the final would kick off at 11am, rather than our normal league 2pm kick-off.

We also found out during these discussions that if we were to win we would become the first team from the Rhondda Valley to have won the Sunday Intermediate Cup. What more incentive did we need?

Prior to the final, though, we had a number of what now seemed like mundane league games to play, which we did, beating the Redgate 4-1, before (ironically considering the semi-final result) losing 9-0 to Maerdy. I dread to think how the Maerdy team felt after this result as it clearly proved they were a far stronger and better side than us, but somehow we had managed to win the semi-final game.

Gutted for Chicky

Even worse than the result for us was the fact that Chicky, who had gone in goal to help us out, broke his leg during the game and would definitely be out for the final. I was gutted, Chicky had played an integral part in getting us to the final. I really felt for him, but it did give me the perfect content for a 'C'mon, lets have 'em and win it for Chicky' speech before the game.

The build-up to the final continued at fever pitch. There was even some talk of everyone having a number one skinhead haircut especially for the final, much like the Romania team did at World Cup in 2014 when they all dyed their hair blond. Luckily this did not take place: my ears are way too big for any of that nonsense.

We all met on the Saturday before the game in the club for a team bonding session, and for the first and only time ever to try to ensure that some of the boys did not drink excessively. When I got to the club, I was confronted by goalkeeper Scabby asking if I could have a word with Chubby, the steward behind the bar, as he would not serve him. Scabby didn't realise this was because I had told Chubby not to serve him. Eventually Scabby's persistence paid off and he got his pint of Bow and black.

Later in the night most of the boys went bowling, to try and overcome any pre-match nerves. I went home. I was too excited thinking about the final to go bowling. Could we become the first Rhondda team to win the Intermediate Cup? I drifted off to sleep.

South Wales Intermediate Cup – final

The morning of the final arrived, and we congregated at the arranged meeting point, outside the florists in Ton Pentre. The bus was already there when I arrived.

I can only assume that Scabby had carried on drinking the Bow at the bowling, as when I talked to him, you could literally smell the booze on him. Never mind, I thought, he'd never let us down before.

Excitement builds as the players, supporters (and the beer) board the bus on our way to the South Wales Intermediate Cup final

It was such a big day, shirts and ties were the designated dress code.

All round good guy Mr Phil Smith was in attendance, capturing the day for us on camera and on film.

We were joined by wives, girlfriends, supporters and even the Club Committee. It really was a big day! There was a great community spirit and huge excitement as we boarded the bus for the journey over the Bwlch mountain road to sunny Maesteg.

Importantly lots of booze was put on the bus as well.

Unsurprisingly we had more players turn up than would fit into the 16-man squad, and I pondered on those that would miss out on the bus trip.

As I thought about the team I would pick, I knew that inevitably there would be disappointment for some. On arriving at the ground, it was clear that we had made more of an effort than the opposition, Cwmafan Pheonix FC, as we outnumbered them four to one in supporters.

The club committee get ready to cheer the boys on in the cup final

The clubhouse on the ground opened as we arrived at 10am and those not involved in the game set about the bar in a positive manner. Unfortunately, their number was increased shortly after when I announced the 16 players to be involved, which meant naming the ones who weren't involved. I felt particularly sorry for Breezy.

That was a hard decision, as everyone wanted to be involved in this game. Those who were involved started to get changed in an excitement-filled dressing room. The sense of excitement increased further when 'Jakey' the club secretary, brought in crates of Carling and Strongbow. My immediate thoughts were that they wouldn't taste very sweet if we lost.

I then gave my 'Let's win it for Chicky/fight them on the beaches/first team from the Rhondda to win this cup' motivational speech. The full speech is on a DVD somewhere if you want a real laugh.

It was after this point that I noticed Scabby, and how rough he was looking. I went over to have a word with him and he was still buzzing with Strongbow. It smelled like he had drunk enough for the whole team. Thinking it would help prior to the game during the warm-up, I took some shots at him. It certainly warmed him up as the sweat was pouring out of him. Only problem was, I think his sweat was 50 per cent Strongbow. I gave him my educated managerial advice: get some water on board and quickly!

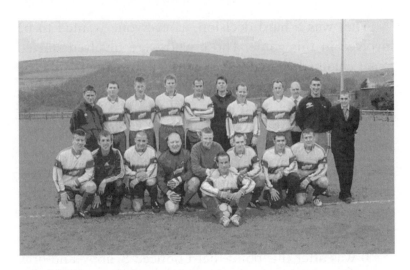

He gulped a good litre down, and said he felt much better.

Only time would tell.

Maindy Con FC before the South Wales Intermediate Cup final:
Back row: Marc Bealo Rees, Peter Roberts, Lewis Thomas, Stuart Smith, Jonny Gardner, Neil Coles, John Evans, Paul Macey, Gareth Voyle, Chris Evans, James Chick (broken leg)
Front row: Matthew Pugh, John Evans, Kris Rees, Simon Jones, Lee Scott, Paul Hughes, Robert Clarke, Ian Lewis

Front: Richard Taylor
Them: Cwmafan Phoenix before the South Wales Intermediate Cup final

The game started at a feverish pace and we were immediately under the cosh as Cwmafan pushed forward. It was instantly clear they were a good, physical team. Our situation was not helped when young Lewis Thomas went off in the first few minutes, with an injury that unfortunately turned out to be a serious ACL (anterior cruciate ligament) one. Thinking fast, I sent on Neil Coles, a tricky winger, but our formation also had to adapt. Not a good start. Despite this setback, we hung on during a turbulent opening 30 minutes defending for our lives.

Then IT happened. Richard 'Tinker' Taylor picked up the ball just outside their penalty area on the right hand side, sidestepping one of their players to give himself a brief bit of space on his favoured left foot. He then opened up his body – and what happened next will live with me for the rest of my life, as Tinker let go a perfectly placed left-foot curler into the top corner of their net. The keeper dived, but he had no chance. Cue massive celebrations, on and off the pitch.

'Get in!' I screamed.

Tinker took off his top to celebrate and twirled it round his head à la Ryan Giggs in the 1999 FA cup semi-final. Sorry, Ryan, but for me, Tinker's goal was even better than yours.

The Cwmafan supporters reacted to the goal – and more specifically the sight of Tinker's chest, with screams of: 'Put you shirt back on!' and 'Chicken-body!'

BUT WE WERE 1-0 UP!

Order was restored, and the game restarted. Despite our great goal, Cwmafan continued to dominate and we were lucky to hang on to our lead until half time. 'Keep going, boys,' I urged them, knowing I could not ask for any more.

It was no surprise, however, when Cwmafan equalised early in the second half. After that, our heads did not go down, but they continued to put us under more and more pressure. Our back four gallantly kept them out until, with about eight minutes of normal time remaining, they had the ball in the back of the net again.

'Offside,' I screamed, standing directly behind the linesman on our side of the pitch. My voice was added to by about another 10 of our lot right behind him, all screaming 'offside' in unison. In truth it looked really tight to me but then, as if in slow motion, the linesman raised his flag for offside. We all breathed a collective sigh of relief. 'Well spotted, lino,' I shouted to him, 'good decision. That was clearly offside'.

We were hanging on and needed support. Club chairman Mr David Ray tried his best repeatedly screaming: 'Mind over matter, boys... mind over matter, boys... we don't mind and they don't matter!' The support raised us and we managed to get to full time level at 1-1.

The boys were knackered, so Choc and I rushed to them with the water bottles. It was up to me to try and get that last bit of effort out of them for the extra time. I tried, but I could sense they already knew how close we were to winning or losing the cup. During the first half of extra time we made a good counter-attack following another of their frequent attacks, which resulted in tricky winger Neil Coles beating their full back before delivering an inch-perfect cross into the heart of their penalty area. Time stood still again as their goalkeeper misjudged the flight of the ball. After what seemed like an age, out of nowhere Ian Lewis rose at the far post to head home in the bottom corner. We were in dreamland. Unsurprisingly Cwmafan refused to lie down, and threw the kitchen sink at us.

I put myself on to waste some time (watching the Premiership had even affected an old goat like myself). The boys at the back were incredible and after what seemed like a lifetime, the referee finally blew his whistle.

We had won the cup!

Most of the boys were out on their feet, kneeling on the floor through sheer exhaustion. This soon passed as the adrenalin and euphoria kicked in on realising what we had achieved. Girlfriends, wives and fans joined us on the field in a celebratory pitch invasion.

A group of close friends from the Rhondda had just won the South Wales Sunday Intermediate Cup. There is no better feeling. I doubt that it could be matched. I would even argue that winning the FA Cup would fall short as it is not normally done with your friends, which is what we were. The famous commentary when Norway beat England in 1981 comes to my mind... Cardiff, Merthyr, Bridgend, Pontypridd, Caerphilly – 'Your boys took hell of a beating!'

Rhondda forever!

Maindy Con FC celebrating winning the South Wales Intermediate Cup, becoming the first team from the Rhondda Valley to do so

Match report from the *Rhondda Leader*

The cup and the individual player winners' medals were presented shortly after the final whistle. No steps to climb up à la Wembley: they were given to us on the side of the pitch. Captain Jonny and I collected and raised the cup in one movement. A loud cheer went up, and in true football fashion we got sprayed with lager (not champagne).

The after-match celebrations started in the dressing room where the cans of Carling and Strongbow were opened and sprayed about. Not too much sprayed about, mind, because it is not every day you get free booze from the Con Club, so most of it was drunk, and drunk very quickly. We then went back into the Maesteg football clubhouse and the feeling could not have been better. I was hugging all and sundry with a massive grin on my face. 'Maindy Con la-la-la' was sung out loud, repeatedly and very boisterously. Everybody was shaking my hand and congratulating me, but I told them all that it was the team had done it.

Hughesy then says to me: 'Guess what Pete... that is the first game on grass we have won all season.' He was right, and what a game to do it in. The trip back to the Con on the bus was a bit of a blur with lots of singing and shouting.

To the tune of 'Kumbaya':

Maindy Con my Lord, Maindy Con,
Maindy Con my Lord, Maindy Con,
Oh Lord Maindy Con.

And of course, the classic to the tune of 'Rocking all over the world':

I like it, I like it, I like it,
I la-la-like it, la-la-like it, here we goooo,

Ton Pentre all over the world!'

'We are the Champions' even got an airing.

When we arrived back at the club, Phil Smith had beaten us back and had set up the video of the game on the TV. We all settled down to watch, pints in hand. There were many oohhs and aahhs watching the game back as the beer flowed. The fun last lasted late into the night and we even did that most Welsh of things: had a good old sing-song.

Celebrations back at the Con

By the end of the evening the actual cup (which we were told we could keep for the year) was being constantly refilled with lager/beer/Guinness and then drunk from. There was no shortage of willing drinking participants.

The management duo with the cup

A real six-pointer

The rest of the season became a bit like after the Lord Mayor's Show.

We lost 5-1 to the Colliers, before losing by the same score to the New Inn.

Due to fixture congestion caused by our cup run (and the strange South Wales FA decision that Sunday League games can only be played on Sundays), the game against the New Inn actually counted for two results and was worth six points to the New Inn. We didn't care: we had just won the cup!

We also lost 3-2 to Treorchy.

For the final game of the season against the Redgate we

drew the starting positions out of a hat. (Perhaps Wenger or Jose Mourinho should try this. You never know – it might work for them.) It resulted in two defenders (Macey and Hughesy) playing up front. Luckily I didn't pull out goalkeeper.

Macey made a case for a striking position the next season by getting his first goal for the club in a game we lost 3-2. In fact, we lost all of our league games after the cup win, and therefore our only win on a grass pitch all season was in the cup final.

Looking back, our second season was an amazing success. Despite us having had a game abandoned in the Rhondda Cup, we then went on to win the South Wales Intermediate Cup, becoming the first-ever team from the Rhondda to win it, doing so by winning our only game on grass all season.

Jakey, the Con Club secretary, sent Phil Smith's photo of us celebrating the cup win on the pitch to the Conservative Club magazine, and we appeared on the front of the next copy!

I bet most of the readers of the Conservative Club magazine had never even heard of the Rhondda Valley before that. Cheekily, I then sent a copy of the Conservative Club magazine to Conservative Party leader Iain Duncan Smith, plus an invitation to our end-of-season presentation night. I also asked if he would sponsor us £80 towards new footballs for next season.

He did not make the presentation night or even sponsor the balls but I did have a nice letter back from his permanent secretary. Despite the snub our end of season presentation night was a great success as not only did we have the normal individual trophies to give out, we also had the actual cup and a cup winning trophy for each player to present.

Like the previous season, I gave a review, before Hughesy gave out the medals.

Maindy Con FC player awards – Season 2:

Players' Player: Jon Gardner

Player of the Year, Most Man-of-the-Match Awards: Kris 'Geesy' Rees

Top Goal Scorer: Ian Lewis

Shortly after the presentation, the management team had another job to carry out... being the DJs. Hughesy and I had been true to our word and were doing the disco. We had made a couple of visits to the electricals shop Maplins and acquired (what we thought) was the necessary gear – although without doubt we would never have been in a position to use it without the far superior skills of Choc, who somehow managed to connect everything to the club's own speakers. How he did this is still a mystery to me.

Choc, you are a better man than me.

I was far more nervous about our DJ-ing than playing in any football game, or giving the presentation season summary. Despite this it was a great disco (I think!)

Well, it was if you liked indie music and classics like the 'Minder' TV theme tune, 'I should be so good for you', sung by Dennis Waterman. This was played at least three times (I know it is a DJ-ing crime to play the same song more than once – but hey, it's a great song), much to the delight of Bealo who was singing and dancing along merrily. The final time it was played, the DJ/management

73

duo themselves ventured off the stage and onto the floor to partake in some wild moves on a heaving dance floor. Mind you, we all looked more like Arthur Daley than Terry McCann. We learned that night that part of the benefit of being the DJ is you can put on what you want when you want.

The South Wales Intermediate Cup then took up pride of place behind the bar in the club for the next 12 months, intermittently taken off its perch to be used as a goblet to drink from.

DJ-ing

The DJ-ing at the presentation night went well and was a great laugh. It must have impressed those in attendance because we somehow became the regular DJs in the club.

Whenever a DJ was needed, we were asked. Soon we were being asked to do a number of 'gigs'. I don't think that our popularity had anything to do with our set list, it was more to do with the fact that we were very cheap. Normally we asked for £20 each, beer money. Generally, I would play the music while Hughesy would get the next songs ready and fend off the queries from the drunken punters.

No easy job.

One or two DJ incidents of note included doing a 60th birthday party for the mother of one of the boys, and it was all going swimmingly until I had used all of my £20 and was a bit worse for wear when Hughesy took a toilet break. I got a bit carried away: I reverted to type and played an old punk classic, 'Pretty Vacant' by the Sex Pistols, pushing the volume up to 11 as I did. I thought it was going down well with all the old dears in attendance, but obviously not, as Hughesy made a hasty return to the decks and cut Johnny Rotten off in full voice.

Another time we were paid in beer cheques... the only problem being, we were not allowed to use any of the beer cheques after the night in question... meaning we had 10 beer cheques each to use all for the same night.

Obviously not wanting to waste any, we set about drinking our 10 pints each in a determined manner. After about 10pm, when we'd had roughly eight pints each, I am not sure what music we played. Lots of punk, I expect.

Season 3

Squad strengthened

We looked forward to the next season with renewed vigour, following our cup success. Many of the other teams in the league felt we had been lucky to win the Intermediate Cup, and it was often stated that we had only triumphed because we had all home draws until the final. Who cares? I thought, nobody could take the achievement away from us.

Let me say it again: Maindy Con South Wales Sunday Intermediate Cup Winner (there, it sounds good); first team from the Rhondda Valley just for good measure as well. Added to the feelgood factor, we strengthened our squad when we signed Owain 'Rooney' Jones. 'Rooney' had been training with us for most of the previous season and as he was now 17 years old he was ready for the adult league. He was a very good player, as he had illustrated during training last season with lightning pace that would definitely aid our cause. Also, as he was not 18, it was a cheap signing: I bought him a packet of crisps. In reality, he should have been playing at a higher level but our cup win had made him keen to sign for the Con.

Con for the League?

With Rooney signing there was even some tentative talk of the Con for the league. What we really needed to do was to start winning games consistently, especially those on grass! If this was to happen then maybe we could have a realistic shot at the league title.

Despite having 10 players out for various reasons, 16 players turned up for the first game of the season against Pentre Rovers. Rooney immediately proved his worth and talent by scoring after 25 seconds into his debut in a man-of-the-match performance. His goal helped us win 3-1.

The next game saw us overcome Ynysmaerdy 2-0. Rooney was on fire, getting another goal and man-of-the-match award. Shame he was too young to have a yard after the game. Bizarrely, their manager approached me at half time to complain about our Astro pitch; his point was that there was too much sand on it, meaning the ball bounced too high. Interesting, I thought, and I actually agreed, but what the hell could I do about it?

Clara Fest

The next game followed the first ever 'Clara Fest' which took place at skipper Gardner's house, in Clara Street, hence the name.

Jonny had set up a makeshift Bierkeller in his back garden, where all of the team and their wives/girlfriends enjoyed an evening of drinking and music. The evening culminated in Jonny and his missus entering the Bierkeller in full Bavarian outfits. It was excellent fun and a brilliant drunken Valleys night, but not the way to prepare for a local derby versus Treorchy the following day. Many of the boys did not get out of their hangover sickbeds to play. Those that did turn up were in a bad way, leading to a terrible performance and an 8-3 reverse, which the Treorchy team were over the moon with. The result dented any title aspirations we had, because in all seriousness in order to win the league you have to win at places like Treorchy.

Our title dreams were firmly extinguished, when we lost our next game 4-1 to Trealaw. The game saw very talented local footballer 'Guppy' play in their team, and to be honest he was a class above everyone else on the field and was instrumental in their victory. Many of the boys were saying after the game that they he could have played at Football League level and I totally agreed.

I found out later that he had played non-league for Newport County.

Hughesy's first goal

The game was also significant for Hughesy, as he broke his Con goal duck. It must have gone to his head as within a couple of minutes he nearly scored again, their keeper scrambling to make an excellent save to deny him a brace. Despite this, somehow or other Hughesy managed to avoid the dreaded yard after the game. He seemed to be very skilled at this.

Our next game was a real battle.

The battle against Silflex

Prior to the game rumours were rife that Silflex, a new team in the league based at a factory in nearby Gilfach Goch, were a tough old bunch. They had previously played in the adjoining Bridgend League, but had joined the Rhondda Sunday League for this season. Rumour had it they had been kicked out of the Bridgend League. Playing them would be fun.

Typically, when we arrived there was no referee. Following a brief discussion that started and ended with, 'Well, we're here now, we might as well play the game', we made a collective decision to play the game with a representative from their team as referee. Things started well and we went ahead early with a well-taken goal from Rooney. From there on things started to go wrong on and off the field.

Firstly, they scored four goals in about 25 minutes. Each of the goals was as silly as the other, from our point of view. At the same time, many vociferous locals came down from the nearby council estate to enjoy the late summer sunshine and consume as much liquid refreshment as they could. Luckily with the score at 4-1, the natives were not restless... this changed, as before half time we fought back, with goals from Geesy and another from Rooney.

Football-wise I was sure we could go on and win it, but in reality I was not really sure I *wanted* us to win, with the ever increasing hostile crowd. Their referee (the father of one of their players) then gave them two debateable penalties and we were further behind. A further goal each meant we were 7-4 down with about 15 minutes left to play. Go on, Wenger, tell me what you would do in this situation.

We started an amazing fight-back with a goal from Geesy. As I celebrated the goal I could hear the words 'Shut up, you dull twat' being shouted at me from the ever-increasing and encroaching bunch of their boys. Having witnessed many hooligan-type scenarios watching Cardiff City – where dancing about with arms wide open and shouting, generally behind the police lines, was the norm – you'd think I would be used to this. But let me tell you, this was a different situation altogether, with no police presence for safety.

Shortly after, Breezy broke through their defence and was bearing down on their goal, when he was hacked down in the box. Unbelievably, their ref gave us a penalty. Ever-calm John Evans stepped up to score it and we were right back in it at 7-6. Geesy then took it upon himself to score with a super header in the far corner, making it 7-7. It was an absolutely brilliant header, but I didn't celebrate.

After our equaliser, the game deteriorated and Silflex's frustrations boiled over. One of their midfielders two-footed John Evans above the knee, before he then tangled with Gardner. Not being shy types, following the tangle Gardner and their player were shortly exchanging punches on the field. The referee sent them both off. Towards the end of the game, I put on the ever-brave (and mad) Jonny Cast. (In truth, he was the only sub who wanted to go on.)

Soon after going on Jonny made a great break down the right wing, but he was suddenly upended, without any of their players in sight. I wondered what had happened to him, as it was difficult to see across the pitch. He later informed me that one of the crowd had tripped him, sending him flying to the floor where he was surrounded by their supporters. His tactic was to laugh; fair enough. I think it was the right decision. The ref eventually blew up and we secured a 7-7 draw, a very hard-fought brave point!

Back in the changing room and the boys were chuffed, but also rushing to get out of there and back to the safety and relative calm of the Con. Only a few of us went back to their club, aptly named 'The Bog', where, to be fair, their team were great with us and we shared a few drinks and food with them.

Soon after the game, Silflex left the league. I never found out if they left voluntarily or were kicked out, but in the end it meant that our hard fought 7-7 draw at the battle of Silflex was not even worth a point!

Losing run

Thoughts of the League title at the start of the season seemed a distant memory as we went on a losing streak, losing 4-2 against the Rhondda Hotel in a game that saw skipper Gardner sent off for the second consecutive game.

This was followed by a very disappointing 4-1 reverse against the Boar's Head. The game saw John Evans complete a clean sweep scoring a goal, gaining the man-of-the-match award, and getting booked. Not many of us decided to go back to the Boar's Head after the game, but for those of us who did, it was an eye-opening experience. Despite it being a Sunday afternoon the place was jumping like a Friday night. It looked like there were people openly skinning up on the bar. I felt quite lame asking for a can of Coke.

We found a quiet(ish) corner at the back of the pub and awaited the obligatory post-match food, looking on in awe at the Sunday afternoon chaos taking place in the rest of the pub. The food was not worth the wait; a tray of curled-up sandwiches.

We were then joined by the local pub character. (I'm sure you have all come across one of these.) Geesy kindly offered him a sandwich from the tray, but we were all taken aback by his sharp reply: 'F**k off. I don't eat.'

He might not eat, but it was obvious he could swig, as with each sup of his beer he downed half a pint. On learning that we are a football team he then went on to tell us that he taught Clive Thomas (the famous – infamous – Welsh referee) everything 'that f**ker knows'. The Boar's Head boys could see him across the pub with us and were laughing away. We ditched the sandwiches and left him talking to himself and taking massive gulps of lager, something I sensed he did very often. The best of British luck to him!

Next up we had our old friends the Railway Inn, but this time we were quietly confident we could beat them for the first time ever. Our confidence stemmed from the fact that we had a very strong team out, and they were missing some important players. Despite this, they still beat us 2-1. I wasn't sure we'd ever beat them.

The next game saw us win our first game on grass since the final last season away to the New Inn, despite it being Jenkins' stag night the night before. Everyone played well and we managed to overcome our grass pitch curse with a 3-2 win.

We then beat Mount Pleasant 2-0 at home, with Rooney getting both the goals.

Normality was restored the following week: we lost 6-1 to Maerdy Hotel. This game saw another local talented footballer, Gareth 'Cod Head' Wharton, play for them. He won all the headers that came near him. No surprise, really, as he is about 6ft 4in tall.

South Wales Intermediate Cup
– round one

Next up we had (yet another) home draw as defending champions in the Intermediate Cup against Ynysmaerdy of the Rhondda League. It was a kind draw against a team from our league, who we had already beaten earlier in the season. Perhaps the South Wales FA liked us for some reason, or maybe we were just lucky.

No bye this year, so we entered the competition in round one. However, any confidence we had was shattered in the club before the game: very unusually our players were low on the ground. Looking at my watch as we were due to leave the club to go to the field I was sure a few more would turn up. But no, they didn't and that day of all days we ended up with only 11 players available, including myself.

Geesy was in attendance, but unfortunately for him and the team he could not play in the competition that year. His Saturday League team had been promoted; as a Welsh League player he was, therefore, ineligible. Dutifully he became the manager for the day, as I was required on the right wing.

Outwardly I remained calm and happy, proclaiming we could win with the 11 players we had, but inwardly I was gutted. After such a great experience in this cup the previous year I felt we should be doing everything we could to do well again. I took a longing glance at the actual cup on the bar as we left the Con on our way to the pitch, fearing it wouldn't be ours for much longer. My fears were soon borne out on the pitch as we found ourselves 2-0 down early in the game. It did not seem like it was going to be our day.

At half time we were still trailing 2-0. I got the boys together in a huddle on the pitch and reminded them that the next 45 minutes were super important if we wanted to have any chance of another great day at out at a final like last season. The message seemed to work. Bealo got a well-taken goal back for us shortly after the break. We then got an equaliser with about 20 minutes left, from Rooney, who was having yet another storming game. It seemed to me as if he was trying to win the game on his own.

Having been involved with us last year, but not part of the team when we won the cup, he seemed to have a strong desire to do well in the cup now that he was part of the team. I imagine he felt that he missed out last year and was desperately trying to recreate another cup run. Personally, all I wanted was either team to score to avoid extra time, because I was knackered! Rooney must have read my mind, because with me out on my arse he turned into a Welsh Thierry Henry, taking on three players before firing home into the bottom corner: an absolutely magic goal, worthy of winning any game. If it had been filmed I am sure it would have won Sky's Wonder Goal competition.

Ynysmaerdy were a team visibly deflated, having been 2-0 up and now losing 3-2. Their discipline started to go. Just before the end there was a clash that left Bealo pole-axed on the floor and rolling about in much pain, it seemed. The perpetrator was correctly sent off. Concerned, I went over to Bealo to check he was all right, but as I got there he winked at me, so I knew there was nothing really wrong with him. He'd been watching too much Premier League. We hung on for a 3-2 win against the odds.

After this game, back in the club as the beers flowed, many of the boys felt that there was something magic about this cup, and I could not agree more. I stayed for a 'quick six' (pints) after the game. They hit me harder than usual because I'd played 90 minutes.

Back to the grind of the league against the Colliers, with ex-Con man Gabby playing for them. We managed (somehow) to stop Gabby from scoring and beat them 2-0.

We then beat the Pentre Labour 4-0 with an interesting line-up that saw Jonny Cast go in goal. As far as I am aware, he is still the only player in Con history who has played a full game in goal and never let a goal in.

South Wales Intermediate Cup – round two

Our next game was the eagerly awaited second round of the SW Intermediate Cup. Amazingly we were drawn at home again. This time we were up against Lewistown Social of the Bridgend League. Prior to the game I had done my managerial homework, finding out that they had beaten Maerdy Social 4-0 in the previous round. As Maerdy were one of the strongest, if not *the* strongest, in our league, it was a great result for them.

I was even more surprised, impressed and concerned when I find out Lewistown actually won 4-0 at Maerdy. Not many teams do that. They were good, very good.

Despite this knowledge, cup fever gripped the club again, especially when Lewistown phoned Hughesy to say that they would be bringing a busload with them and staying for food and drinks after the game. True to their word, they turned up on the day in a 25-seater, and with our supporters there was a good crowd present.

The game started with them well on top forcing a number of corners, but we defended well to keep them out. Brad and Gardner were particularly strong at the back. As the game progressed, we started to create the better chances, but it was 0-0 at half time. I gave my 'Come on, lads' speech, explaining to them that if we scored and they didn't, we'd win. (Simple really – that is the essence of football at any level – what do you need to be paid millions and have coaching badges for?)

They had the benefit of a strong wind in the second half, but we created the better chances. The deadlock was finally broken when Ian Lewis calmly tucked one away with a sweet finish with his left foot. Lewistown continued to push for the equaliser but we were always dangerous on the counter-attack. Following one such counter, Rooney broke away towards goal. Their keeper rushed out and made a great one-handed save, pushing the ball away from Rooney's feet. We thought the keeper looked close to being outside the box. The referee agreed and gave us a free kick.

We would have been happy with that, but very harshly the referee showed a red card in the direction of their keeper. Lewistown were incensed, and surrounded the referee; then one of them called him (rather impolitely) a cheat. Unsurprisingly, he got his marching orders as well, and they were left with only nine men on the field and also trying to find a replacement keeper. We should have been well on top, but the game became scrappy and surprisingly it was Lewistown who created a number of chances. Then there was a clash in the centre circle between Evo and their midfielder, resulting in Evo and their player wrestling on the floor. They were both, correctly, yellow-carded, but as their player had been carded before, he was off. They were left with eight men.

At this point, I felt that it might be a good time to enter

the fray, a calm head to see the game out. Shortly before the end of the game, I somehow managed to find the net (from 25 yards, I might add) and the game was safe at 2-0.

Despite an obviously disappointing result and outcome for them, all the Lewistown boys came back to the club. Sportingly, there were no sour grapes in relation to the result or the three red cards they received. I was convinced that without the red cards the result may well have gone against us, adding to the general feeling that this cup was magic.

The Lewistown boys soon forgot about the result and tucked straight into the post-match drinking. They were the first team to beat us at a drinking game, and also introduced us to new drinking games. One particular new drinking game they brought to the table is called Jacks. It involves participants turning playing cards over one after the other, and results in one person drinking lots, along these lines:

> If you turn over the first of the jack cards, then you pay for the drink.
>
> If you turn over the second jack card, then you decide on the drink.
>
> If you turn over the third jack card, then you have to fetch the drink from the bar.
>
> And finally, if you turn over the fourth jack, then you get to drink the drink.

The sense of excitement when there is only the last jack to reveal caused much merriment over and over, particularly as Bealo went on a losing run of three in a row.

Double whiskies were the popular choice of the day. Consequently, and unsurprisingly, Bealo was steaming drunk. As his drunkenness increased his speech became more slurred; the Lewistown boys on hearing his name thought he was saying Booboo, not Bealo. That was enough for all of us. Up went the 'Booboo! Booboo!' shout. It resounded around the lounge every time Bealo/Booboo got up on to his increasingly unsteady feet.

That Jacks game has a lot to answer for.

The Lewistown boys had such a good laugh that they cancelled their bus and arranged a later one. They joined us down the road for further drinking at the New Inn and Fagins. We gave them a good send-off when their bus arrived; many of the boys have remained friends since the game.

Back to the league

We took our good cup form into the league with good wins against Treorchy and the Anchor. These were followed up with hard-fought draws against the Redgate and the Railway Inn.

The draw against the Railway was the first time in three seasons we had taken any points from them and was a big achievement. However, as we were 2-0 up at half time, it was disappointing to end up with a draw. I doubted we would have a better chance to beat them.

We were in good spirits for exactly the same fixture against the Railway Inn the following week in the Rhondda Cup. We should not have been, mind, as normal service against the Railway was resumed and we lost 9-0. And we were lucky to get nil.

We lost our next game 6-4 against the Anchor: a poor

result and not very good preparation for the quarter final of the South Wales Intermediate Cup.

South Wales Intermediate Cup – quarter final

We were drawn at home again (this is getting silly now) against fellow Rhondda League team the New Inn. They were very similar in standard to us, so before the game my thoughts were that we could win but then so could they. Our cause was not helped by skipper Jonny Gardner going away on holidays. John Evans was given the armband for the day, something I had no qualms over. I was confident he would do an excellent job.

John won the toss and decided to play against a strong wind in the first half. The decision looked to be the correct one. The New Inn were pumping everything in the air and the ball was either running away with the wind straight out for a goal kick, or John and Evo were winning them in the air with big headers. It was the New Inn, however, who broke the deadlock, putting themselves 1-0 up. I could see the confidence drain from the boys.

But then, totally against the run of play, Matthew Pugh sent one of his lethal long throws into the box and Stuart Smith caught it perfectly on the volley from the penalty spot into the corner of the net. The keeper had no chance. This would have been special enough, but the fact Stuart did this with his right foot (I don't think I'd ever seen Stuart kick the ball right-footed before) was even more spectacular.

The goal changed the complexion of the game and the momentum swung in our favour. Not long afterwards, after another long throw from Matthew Pugh, Rooney was in with a chance and he didn't disappoint, racing past the central defender before lobbing over the keeper as if he wasn't there. The New Inn piled the pressure on us, but just before half time Rooney dispossessed the last defender, took the ball into the box and side-footed it into the net.

At the break there was much happiness and excitement in our pitch side huddle, but I dampened it somewhat by reminding the boys that nothing was won yet, and that the New Inn would want it big time, second half. I even gave some tactical advice: play it on the floor, because playing it in the air with the wind at our backs wouldn't work, as it hadn't for the New Inn in the first half.

Early in the second half Bealo nearly scored the goal of the season with a volley that their keeper saved well. Bealo has always maintained he is the best volleyer in the club and he nearly proved it. From the resulting corner the ball came to the edge of the area, where Hughesy popped it back hopefully goalwards with his right foot. The wind caught the ball, and somehow it sailed over the keeper and into the net. What was happening?

Firstly Stuart Smith scored a goal with his right foot; now another one from the even more left-footed Hughesy. We then got a corner. Ian Lewis said to me (on the touchline) as he prepared to take the kick: 'I'm going to put this straight in using the wind' – and guess what... he did it! The New Inn lost some of their discipline, but they did manage to get a goal back and also forced Lee into making two excellent saves. Just before the final whistle, to calm any nerves Bealo put Rooney through, who finished neatly for his hat-trick.

Rooney was almost single-handedly taking us through to each round of the cup: we reached the semi-final for the second year running. Back in the club, the result was excitedly and drunkenly relayed to Gardner on his holidays. We told him to hurry home as we had got another semi-final to prepare for. Our preparation was hindered, however, as our next four League games were cancelled because of a combination of lack of referees and bad weather.

South Wales Intermediate Cup – semi-final

This did not give us any chance to prepare for the semi-final – amazingly, we were drawn at home again. Our opponents were Pentwyn DC of the Cardiff and District League. Cardiff teams are always strong but previous knowledge informed me they don't like coming to play in the Valleys, meaning the home draw was key again.

In the morning, despite our 'all weather' pitch, there was some doubt over the fixture, as we'd had an unseasonal dusting of snow, but prior to kick-off the sun came out and the snow melted. In fact, when the referee arrived he seemed more concerned by the penalty spots on the lovely Astro than the fast-disappearing snow. I tried to explain to him that both the penalty spots had been burned out and replaced so many times that the divots around them were a constant rather than a temporary issue. He was not convinced by this explanation, and was even considering calling the game off. I then told him if he called the game off, the penalty spots (and the divots around them) would be exactly the same the next week. He reluctantly gave in and agreed to the game going ahead. I think he just took pity on us and how shit our pitch was.

Pentwyn DC missed all of these pitch discussions as they turned up very late, at 1.35pm. Apparently, they got lost trying to find us, just like everyone from Cardiff does when they have to go further north than Pontypridd.

Everybody was fit, and we had a full squad and were ready to go. The game started at a fast pace. Pentwyn were on top, sending the ball up front repeatedly, but Jon and John were strong at the back. Lee was forced to make two good saves, with one shot skidding up in front of him and one from a free kick. We eventually got into the game. Macey was strong on the right-hand side. Ian and Rooney were causing problems for their back four, which very unusually included identical twin brothers.

The first half ended goalless.

The second half started unbelievably: they cut us apart from the kick-off and ended up with a clear strike on goal, which hit the post and we breathed a sigh of relief. It looked like one goal would nick it, but who would get it? It turned out to be us: following good work down the right Rooney stole a yard and squared it to Ian who finished well. Our goal was scored with only 11 minutes remaining. Could we hang on and reach another final?

As Graham Taylor used to say, 'Do I not like that' when, with only three minutes left, their striker, who had had an excellent game, got a chance which he somehow managed to scoop over Lee from the most acute angle. The ball rolled agonisingly into our net.

The referee blew and the game finished 1-1. Going into extra time the momentum was definitely with Pentwyn.

During the second half of extra time, just as I am starting to think about who will be taking at least five penalties for us, Ian set up Rooney, and it was a straight race between him, the centre back and the keeper. I should not have been surprised as Rooney won the race and calmly flicked the ball over their keeper and coolly headed it into the empty net. Top quality striking at any level. Do I like that? Yes!

We managed to hang on for the final eight minutes, which seemed to take an age, but eventually the referee put us out of our misery and we sealed a 2-1 extra time win. We were going to the South Wales Intermediate Cup final for the second year in a row. With home draws all along the way! The changing room was buzzing with excitement and everyone was congratulating Rooney on his fantastic winning goal. He could now enjoy the final, having not been involved in last seasons.

Maindy make final

■ FOOTBALL

Maindy Con FC 2
Pentwyn 1

MAINDY Con Football Club reached the final of the South Wales Intermediate Sunday Cup, beating Pentwyn 2-1 in a tense semifinal match.

Pentwyn started the game brightly and put the Maindy goal under pressure during the first 20 minutes.

Maindy played some good football, with Marc Rees and Chris Evans prominent in the midfield.

The Rhondda club started to dominate, with Paul Hughes and Stuart Smith working well and Paul Green and Paul Macey influential.

The deadlock was finally broken with 10 minutes remaining when Maindy striker Owain Jones created space and unselfishly squared the ball to Ian Lewis who coolly finished from 12 yards out.

During the final 10 minutes, Pentwyn threw everything at the Maindy defence and they were rewarded with an equaliser three minutes from time.

With the score 1-, the game went to extra time.

With both teams thinking of penalties, Maindy man-of-the-match Owain Jones broke free of the Pentwyn defence to score the winning goal.

Maindy Con Football Club can now look forward to the final, which will take place in April.

Maindy make final

All I was hoping for was a similar result.

The Pentwyn team came back to the club, before their long trip back to the little big smoke (Cardiff). Due to the numbers in attendance we used the function room upstairs for the after-match analysis, food and celebration. After a few pints, I said to Rooney that his winning goal was one of the best I had witnessed in such a pressure game and environment. The Pentwyn team left and the pints were sunk rapidly, another quick six being the order of the day. Get another round in, Pete! Talk centred on the fact that we had another cup final to look forward to.

Back to the league, and much like last season we lost our way before the final, losing 5-1 at home to Maerdy and then 2-1 away to the Colliers. It was obvious to everyone that all our thoughts were too much on the cup final. The Colliers game was as competitive as ever, and very unusually, never having made a tackle in my life, I was involved in a flashpoint. It erupted when I was cynically brought down just outside their box. Their player was adamant I dived and forcefully let me know, as I slowly got up off the grass. Not being an aggressive type, I was a little concerned as he came closer, screaming and shouting, telling me that I effing dived. The flashpoint was soon over: he backed off rapidly when Gardner came over to sort it out. Thank you, skipper! From the resultant free kick my shot was saved (old school rules – I took the free kick as I was fouled) but their keeper only parried it out to Hughesy, who steadied himself before tapping it in. Despite this we lost the game 2-1. It was not a very good preparation for the final.

South Wales Intermediate Cup – final

The final was to be played at Treforest Football Club, against Pentwyn FC. They were a different team from the same area of Cardiff as our semi-final opponents. Some of you may have heard of Treforest: it is the hometown of the legendary singer Sir Tom Jones. I wonder if Sir Tom has ever graced the pitch? Perhaps I should write and ask him one day – unless you are reading, Tom? If so let me know.

The venue was chosen by the powers that be in the SWFA as it was midway between us and our opponents. Hughesy had been busy again and had arranged a bus for the team and our supporters. This time, though, it was a double-decker!

Despite a change in bus, I was hoping for the same result as last year. Unfortunately, for us as a team and for them individually, Geesy and Tinker were not eligible to play. They were both playing in the Welsh League on a Saturday, and therefore ineligible for this cup. Again, I had to let some of the boys down when I named the 16-man squad.

The game started well, with us on top. We got a free kick on the edge of the box, which unfortunately came to nothing. But I felt the momentum was with us, especially as we were being roared on by a vociferous crowd – including some of the boys from the Treorchy Prince of Wales team who had come to support us. A nice gesture, which was appreciated by us.

However, it was Pentwyn who got the first goal. We nearly got back in it immediately when Stu Smith struck the post with a wicked long-range effort. Unfortunately they started to boss the game, and they scored again before half time. We were definitely up against it. I told the boys at half time that we had 45 minutes to salvage the cup. The second half started badly with Evo going off injured; the referee eventually had enough of Ian Lewis who has been niggling him throughout the game, and he was eventually sent off. I warned Ian about this at half time but the red mist had already descended.

The final nail in our coffin came when Rooney went off with a suspected broken ankle and they wrapped the game up with another two well-taken goals. I went on for the final 15 minutes, which turned out to be an incident-packed period. Firstly, John Evans almost grabbed a consolation for us, which would have been deserved. Secondly, for the only time in my career I was asked by the Treorchy boys to do the Ayatollah, a Cardiff City fans craze which saw everyone banging their head repeatedly with their hands. This cheered me up no end – cheers, boys! Finally, and most bizarrely (but not surprisingly to us) the game was interrupted by a streaker. When he bounded onto the field it was not immediately clear to me who it was, from my place on the pitch, but I should have guessed. It was no other than Jonny Cast.

Stark naked, he burst onto the field and went straight up to the Pentwyn bench where he performed a drunken, naked jig in front of them. They looked confused and bemused. He then ran over to the referee and performed the same jig in front of him – before planting a kiss on his cheek. It was clear that their bench and the referee did not see the funny side of it. Jonny followed these stunts up with a couple of roly-polies as he left the field to loud cheers, laughs and roars from our supporters.

Soon after the streaker excitement, the final whistle put us out of our misery and our incredible run in the Intermediate Cup was over. There was much heated debate in the dressing room after the game as many of the boys' suspected that Pentwyn had played players from too high a league: in other words, ineligible players.

'Pete, you should report them.'

'We should have the cup by default'.

'You should have played Geesy and Tinker!'

To be honest this was more stressful than the game itself. I took a philosophical stance on it: the better team beat us and if they had cheated then so be it. The only nagging thought in my mind was that Geesy and Tinker would have made a huge difference for us if they had played.

After the game things calmed down and we went back to the Treforest Club, conveniently located on the ground. Despite winning the cup the Pentwyn team only stayed for one drink before heading back. We were left to drown our sorrows among ourselves. The game was soon forgotten as the drink flowed. On the bus back there was a vastly different atmosphere to last year and Hughesy dropped a bombshell, explaining that he was done as part of the management team. One more season, I told him, one more season. 'We'll see', he said. It looked like I had got a job on my hands keeping the management team together... or perhaps he was just gutted after losing the final.

Streaker – letter from SWFA

A couple of days after the final, as we were still mulling over the decision whether or not to appeal that Pentwyn used ineligible players, we received an alleged misconduct letter from the South Wales FA in relation to Jonny Cast's streak. We were being charged with FAW Rule 24.12 and South Wales FA Rule 25, namely 'Acting in a way likely to bring the game into disrepute', in respect of our club supporter. Added to the letter was the match referee's report and he was obviously not happy.

In it he stated: 'It is with regret I advise of an incident which occurred during the above game. Having signalled the restart following an award of a throw-in to Pentwyn, I had cause to halt play due to an outside agent entering the field of play in a state of undress.

'The agent, allegedly associated with Maindy Conservative Club, entered the field of play and proceeded to run to the opponents' dug-out area, in a jovial but provocative manner. Furthermore, prior to his departure from the field of play, the agent ran towards me, grabbed my arm and embraced me in a clench and placed a kiss on my right cheek.'

We composed a reply to the charge, stating that we could not be responsible for the behaviour of people who turned up to watch the game, wherever they came from – in other words completely denying any knowledge of Jonny! Luckily for us the charge was dropped, but it ended any thoughts of us reporting Pentwyn for using ineligible players.

The cup was lost.

The season ended with some mundane games including a 4-2 win against the Rhondda Cup winners New Inn. The game was played in very un-Valleys-like warm weather, a fierce heat – and was the first and only time I have been involved in a game where the referee stopped after 25 minutes of each half for water breaks.

Our penultimate game of the season saw us draw 3-3 each away to Ynysmaerdy. Ian Lewis bagged a brace, and I managed to get one. It leaves Ian and Rooney on 20 goals each with one game of the season remaining.

The final game of the season saw us beat the Rhondda

Hotel 3-2 and with Rooney through on goal he seemed destined to be top scorer, but unselfishly he squared the ball to Ian, who tapped home. This was a great magnanimous gesture as it meant Ian pipped him to Top Goal Scorer by one goal.

Maindy Con FC player awards – Season 3:

Players' Player of the Year: Jon Gardner

Player of the Year: Owain Jones

Top Goal Scorer: Ian Lewis

Our presentation night was made memorable for me, as the club and the boys had got together to get me a fetching black 'Maindy Con' fleece, so I now nearly had a big manager's coat.

Season 4

PRIOR TO OUR fourth season I delved into the transfer market once again, signing the Butler brothers (Gareth and Andrew), Michael Davies (aka Bobby) and Craig Pugh. We also re-signed club character Gabby.

Welsh International

We also signed former Boys' Clubs of Wales international Steve Hughes. He was also a former Ton Pentre Welsh League player.

So at last we had an international in our squad! The only problem was that Steve was even older than me. Despite this I knew Steve would be a good addition and, more importantly, he was a regular drinker in the club and a punk rocker. Our final summer signing was Darren White – 'the Mighty White'. Darren had been an excellent youth player who had not quite made the step up to the level many people felt he should have; he would definitely be an asset to us.

With our signings on board, again confidence was high and we felt we might be able to have a shot at the title.

The season started with an away trip to Rhondda Hotel in the late beautiful August summer sunshine. The weather reminded me why I have long been an advocate of grassroots football in Wales being a summer sport;

starting the season at Easter and playing throughout the summer. This is not only because the weather is nicer in the summer, but also because so many games are called off during the winter. In the current set-up there is always a regular fixture congestion in April/May anyway. This congestion undermines the meritocracy of local leagues as many teams struggle to put a strong team out for the many rearranged mid-week fixtures.

Teams sometimes have to play on a Tuesday and Thursday night and then the Saturday as well. With kick-off times often at 6pm for the weekday matches, it prevents many players participating in these games because of work commitments. This causes weakened teams for these end-of-season fixtures, and the results are affected.

I can only see benefits for summer football, as the weather and therefore the pitches, would be better, and the league outcomes more accurate and reflective. It could also possibly result in producing better, more technical football on the improved pitches. The only argument I could see against this is that it would clash with the cricket season. But could league cricket be played on a Sunday? Food for thought. Back to the game and despite the sun (or even because of the sun) we won the game 3-2 win thanks to goals from Gabby, Tinker and Steve Hughes, with a goal on his debut.

A home local derby versus Treorchy was next and despite dominating the game, we lost 1-0 to a hotly disputed penalty. Nigel, the former manager of the Railway Inn, awarded it: following his retirement from playing and managing, he had become a local referee. He was giving something back to the league he used to play and manage in. Considering Nigel was aware of the abuse the referees receive, his taking up the role was even more impressive. However, I could not stop myself from thinking that perhaps Nigel was thinking of his previous battles with us when he gave Treorchy the decisive penalty.

Next up we beat the RAFA Club 2-0 at home, with super Gabby notching again. The game saw goalkeeper Lee Scott come on as an outfield player. You know what goalkeepers are like, always telling you (and everyone) else that they can play out. So here was Lee's big chance to show everyone; he promptly got sent off after about a minute on the field. Let that be a lesson to all goalkeepers out there: despite what Guardiola may think, you are not outfield players for a reason.

Stick to the goal.

Referee but no whistle

The referee-shortage issue threatened our next game against the Baden Powell Club. The game went ahead when both teams and management agreed to play the game with one of their boys refereeing this time. However, the situation was even worse than normal, if that is possible, as the designated referee did not even have a whistle.

Picture the scene: a non-qualified referee, taking charge of the game with no whistle, literally shouting for decisions. A recipe for chaos. It was ridiculous, and I was fuming when Ian Lewis scored a header from outside the box (a great goal) but it was only after he finished celebrating that we realised the 'ref' had 'shouted' to disallow the goal. For what I still have no idea. Despite this crazy situation we managed to win 5-3, and even though the boys, particularly Ian, moaned about the ref's performance, I actually thought he did quite well under the circumstances.

I have no doubt that Mourinho would not have agreed to the game, but it is a necessity in local football.

Our curse on grass continued against the New Inn as we lost 2-0 away to them, in a game where we missed a penalty in the last minute with the score at 0-1. Typically they then went down the other end and wrapped things up with a second goal.

Ref shortage

The ref shortage in the League became even worse, and two of our next three games took place without referees. Despite this, we managed to beat a determined Tylorstown Rovers team 3-2, before losing to the Rhondda Hotel Porth.

Finally, we got a referee, and beat the Three Horse Shoes 4-0 at home.

Our next fixture saw us lose to the Ynyscynon (previously the Colliers – now playing from a different pub) 4-2 in a game that saw Brad get his first-ever red card as he was sent off for a handball on the line.

It was a great save!

The game, however, ended on a sour note as on returning to the changing rooms it became apparent that they had been broken into during the game. Unfortunately, lots of stuff had been pinched from both teams, including money and clothes. They did not steal my shell-suit mind, so I was relieved. (Mark my words, shell-suits were all the rage at one time. I'd just never moved on.)

From this incident onwards, we decided to take a 'valuables' bag out with us during future games. In the bag (or sock in some cases) everyone puts in their money, keys, phones etc, and then the bag does not leave our side during the game. A sad but necessary solution. I bet this does not happen to Harry Kane and his ilk in the Premier League.

The Mighty White netted in a 1-1 draw with the Anchor in the next game that saw Brad and Evans in caretaker manager roles once again. The draw meant they were still undefeated in their caretaker manager roles, and boy, did they let everyone know in the club after the game.

In the first round of the Rhondda Cup we then beat the New Inn, current Rhondda Cup holders, 3-2, with Gabby, continuing his good form, scoring the winning goal.

Next up was the big one, as South Wales Intermediate Cup fever took hold again. We were drawn away to Litchard Park from the Bridgend League in the first round. Despite this being our third season in the cup, it was our first ever away draw. It was a tough assignment, but we were in buoyant mood as we set off from the club, over Bwlch mountain to Bridgend in a hastily-arranged minibus.

Darren White, I was told, was well up for the game today. 'Darren is going to snap a few of them today.' Darren duly delivered, with two goals and a man-of-the-match performance, in a 4-2 victory that also included a goal from Hughesy that hit the stanchion from the edge of the box.

Hughesy celebrated with an 'Ayatollah' Cardiff City celebration, which wound up the Jacks on their team. I never knew there were Jacks in Bridgend but it seems there are. After the game, we joined the Litchard team back at their clubhouse, conveniently right on their ground. The drinking games started; they were no match for us in this department either. This Intermediate Cup was magic.

No parkie

Our next game was cancelled, despite there being two teams and a referee present. This time there was no park-keeper there to open the changing rooms. Both teams were happy to get changed on the side of the pitch, and play without nets, but the referee saw sense and decided to call the game off.

Not bad for a centre half, John Evans scored two and was man-of-the-match in a 2-1 win versus the RAFA Club in our next fixture. The winning goal he scored was a 30-yard screamer against well-respected and renowned local keeper Tim Mellor in the RAFA goal.

We then beat the Rhondda Hotel Ferndale 6-1, with the Mighty White getting four goals and Andrew Butler got his debut Con goal.

We got our first-ever point in four seasons against Maerdy in a 1-1 draw, that saw Bobby and I both miss good chances to sneak it at the end of the game. Winning would have been unbelievable.

Another Darren White hat-trick helped us beat Tylorstown Rovers 6-0 and we powered up to third in the League.

Darren then bagged a brace as we beat the Baden Powell 4-0, in which Craig Pugh scored his first goal for the club.

South Wales Intermediate Cup – round two

In a repeat of the semi-final from two seasons ago we were

drawn at home to Maerdy. If anything, the two teams were more even now than they were two years ago, when despite our win they were a far stronger team than us. I sensed before the game that they were very determined to beat us, but we were quietly confident following our recent draw with them in the league. The game was a very tight affair and was a 0-0 stalemate at half time. They seemed to be getting frustrated and we were not, so at half time I was optimistic of progressing. As often is the case the first goal was going to be crucial.

Unfortunately, they got that crucial first goal, and then went on to beat us 2-0 in a game that could have gone either way. It was our first loss (outside of the losing final last season) in this competition in the three years we had taken part. Although the boys were deeply disappointed, it was a statistic to be proud of.

No surprises next: we lost 4-1 to the Railway again, continuing our terrible run against them.

What's the score?

With 20 minutes of our next fixture against Ynyscynon remaining, I was required as the last available substitute. This was unexpected as we had four subs, two of whom had gone on, but the other had to leave, meaning I was now required. I had to make a hasty dash to the changing rooms to get my shin pads. At the time we were losing 1-0. I then entered the field of dreams, and was delighted when Geesy scored a wonderful goal for us. We nearly got another one, but the game ended 1-1.

Back in the changing room, I was congratulating all the boys, delighted with our hard-earned point. It was only when I went to the referee's room to get the match card signed that I realised that we had actually lost 2-1, Ynyscynon having scored when I was putting my shin pads on! I was convinced we had drawn the game, and was gutted to have lost. The boys didn't help, mercilessly ribbing me about my miscalculation. 'You senile old sod,' was the general consensus.

We had an identical fixture the following week in the eagerly anticipated quarter final of the Rhondda Cup. I thought we had a good chance of progressing as last week was a close game... so close I thought it was a draw. I was not that happy to see Stuart Jones refereeing, especially after his antics in our abandoned game a few seasons ago. As expected the game was close, but we went 1-0 down late in the first half. Shortly after the break Macey equalised with a great long-range goal, and it was game on!

As the game was coming to a close, we were under the cosh as Ynyscynon pushed for a winner. According to my watch, however, time was up and I was thinking about getting the boys together and regrouped in the stoppage before extra time. But Stuart kept on playing and playing.

Unusually I got annoyed and I sent him a verbal volley of abuse, which he definitely heard as he told me politely to shut up. I thought managers were meant to shout at referees, not the other way around. Stuart kept on playing and playing and then the inevitable happened: after a goal-mouth scramble, Ynyscynon got the winning goal. Within a second of the restart Stuart put the whistle to his mouth, blew up, and we are out of the cup. I've heard of Fergie-time, but this was more like 'let's play until the Con lose time'.

We got over this disappointment with a resounding 12-0 dismantling of Ynysmaerdy, Rooney getting six goals and the Mighty White four.

The Mighty White was at it again with a hat-trick next against Rhondda Hotel Porth in a 4-3 victory. That result was followed up with a hard-earned 2-1 away at the Three Horse Shoes.

Having beaten Ynysmaerdy 12-0 a couple of weeks ago, you would have thought the away game would have been a stroll in the park. If this fixture had been on the betting coupons we would have been nailed on.

Think again.

Despite being awarded an early penalty, which we gave to Brad, all of us hoping that he would get his first goal for the Con in an 'easy fixture'. Unfortunately Brad missed the penalty. It is as if we had upset the football gods: we were then dragged into a close game. As you can imagine, they were very keen to avenge their 12-0 stuffing and there were some meaty challenges going in. Lee then made a fumble in the last minute, allowing them in to pinch a 1-0 victory. To say they enjoyed it immensely would be an understatement. If I listen carefully I think I can still hear them celebrating now. You would have thought they had won the FA Cup.

To be honest I sniggered: the irony of a 12-0 victory turning into a 1-0 loss to the same team a few weeks later perfectly highlights the craziness of football at this level.

Disallowed goal

Next up we lost the local derby 3-2 against Treorchy in a game that referee Philip Jones (a good friend of mine) disallowed a goal I scored. As I don't score many goals, to say I was not impressed would be putting it mildly.

Despite my protestations, Phil was convinced that Geesy was in an offside position at the same time as I coolly slotted home from 12 yards out. Phil, if you are reading this, I swear it was onside! Geesy was not interfering with play and therefore the goal should have stood. The game was also memorable as it saw a debut for the Con Club chairman, Mr Mike Eggert, four years after he and the committee agreed to help sponsor the team.

We lost our next fixture 4-2 to the New Inn, in a game that the referee stopped with 15 minutes to play because he had an injury (or did he want to get away early once he had been paid?), but unfortunately for us the result stands.

Our nemesis the Railway were up next, and normality returns as they beat us 9-1. It was only 2-1 with 15 minutes to go. I thought we had passed, letting in seven goals in the last 15 minutes, but obviously not.

The Tour – Ashby-de-la-Zouch

THE HIGHLIGHT AT the end of our fourth season was our first-ever tour. We were going abroad – well, to England – Ashby de la Zouch in Leicestershire, to play against Ashby Town FC. It was the first (and last to date) time I have played football in England. However, never mind *playing* football there: this would be the first time some of the boys had even *been* to England!

I organised the tour with a great friend of mine, Adrian Sheehan, who I had met at university. He was the esteemed goalkeeper for Ashby Town FC. The organisation was not straightforward; it never is, trying to get 20-odd boys organised and arranged with transport and hotel rooms. They were more like girls arguing over who would be sharing a room with who. It required many, frequent 'tour meetings' in the Con, where we started off discussing arrangements and ended up getting pissed. 'Will I need my passport, Pete?' was a genuine question I was asked. Everyone was up for it.

I really appreciated the fact that Adrian did lots of the organising at his end, including arranging the pitch and the referee. He even went the extra mile and bought a cup, and so the game was to be played for the inaugural and aptly named Anglo-Welsh Cup.

Although the 52-seater bus was not quite full, there was much excitement and anticipation as we boarded at the Con at 9am sharp, Saturday morning. The driver Dorian and his co-driver Sid would be staying in Ashby overnight on Saturday, before driving us back on the Sunday, hopefully with the Anglo-Welsh Cup on board. Those boys present but not playing later in the day set about the booze on the bus as soon as we pulled off from Ton Pentre.

After a long, warm, four hours on the bus (great preparation for the game, I must say) we arrived in Ashby. Those who had started drinking as we left were by now in a bit of a mess.

Dorian and Sid located the ground and dropped all of us plus our kit/overnight bags off near the ground. Ashby is not a huge town and, as a result, we had booked into three different hotels/bed and breakfasts. Some of the boys were getting concerned that they had not seen their hotel. I reassured them by informing them that some places are bigger than Ton Pentre!

Before the game kicked off we lost four of our supporters (Lemo/Big Neil/Patrick and Choc) to the pub. They were very wise, if you ask me. It was a very warm day and they were heading straight for a beer garden.

I met up with Adrian and told him that the facilities at the ground were impressive, far better than we were used to. So they should be: we were playing abroad.

Soon the banter started... 'Come on lads, we gotta beat these English bastards' echoed around our changing room – just loud enough for their boys to hear in the next changing room.

I went and met Adrian and his team. I could sense that despite the good nature, they wanted to beat us. I'm sure I heard 'These Welsh bastards are taking the mick' as I left.

Game on! It felt more competitive than a tour game.

We're Up for the Cup

Ashby, using their home advantage, and utilising the fact that we had not settled into the English atmosphere, started the game on top. They almost took an early lead following a fumble by makeshift keeper Ian Lewis, who had gone in goal as no keeper had come on the tour with us. Luckily for us, following the fumble, the striker's shot hit the post before rebounding to safety. We all breathed a sigh of relief.

Ashby Town FC before the inaugural Anglo/Welsh Cup game

After that shock start we settled and adjusted to playing in a different country. Now we knew how Gareth Bale felt when he first played in Spain, acclimatising to the different conditions. The deadlock was broken when a good cross from Andrew Butler fell to his brother Gareth, who confidently tucked away his first goal for the club off his shin pad. Gareth celebrated wildly, even taking his shirt off and waving it in the air. His actions heated up the atmosphere, on an already boiling day.

Soon after, Macey doubled our advantage with a well-taken goal. Just before half time John Evans rose like a salmon to plant a header in the far corner to leave their keeper, my mate Adrian, pawing at thin air. We were coasting, 3-0 up at half time.

The second half started in even warmer weather, and

the game slowed down considerably. Michael Davies (aka Bobby) then scored his first goal for the club after good work by Craig Pugh and the game was all over as a contest. Rooney, as ever, got his goal near the end and we ended up the 5-0 winners – 5-0 was a bit harsh on them, but it was nice for the Con to get our first win on foreign soil (and it was on grass!).

Claiming the inaugural Anglo-Welsh Cup

After the game, our changing room was very loud with Welsh singing: we are famous for it, after all. In fairness, the Ashby team took it really well. Following a quick shower we were all ready for the night ahead. After a brief visit to the various hotels to drop off our bags, we were out into the bright lights of Ashby for the night. Would they know what was about to hit them?

Our first port of call was the pub that our 'supporters' had been at all day. They were very surprised but quite pleased to hear that we'd won the Anglo-Welsh Cup, but by the look of them, they'd had a much better time in the pub.

The drinking games started soon after, carried out in the bright sunshine in the pub's pleasant beer garden. The first game to get an airing was 'Ps and Ss'. This is a word association game, where you are not allowed to say any words that start with either the letter 'P' or the letter 'S'. It sounds simple, but let me tell you after a couple of pints it is more difficult that you think, especially when you are lined up by experienced players with words like 'carrot'. Most people respond to 'carrot' with 'pea' – meaning they lose and are punished by drinking. Often when the game is in full swing and the beer has already flowed, you even get boys *starting* the game with a P or an S word.

The penalty for that misdemeanour is a 'full-pint bolter'. It was clear that not many of the Ashby boys knew how to play this game and they were rightly reluctant to join in. Perhaps this had more to do with the fact that they could clearly see that there were a number of fish (big drinkers) in among our lot – none more so than the skipper himself, Jonny Gardner, who was our regular drinking games chairman/master of ceremonies.

Knowing my lack of drinking prowess and my poor track record with drinking games I sneaked off, leaving them to it, and headed back in to the pub. I passed the time discussing the game with the Ashby boys, who were actually quite impressed with our team, telling me that we would be able to hold our own in their league. I felt a great sense of pride knowing this.

The relative peace in the pub was soon interrupted

by the boys coming in from the beer garden in full Welsh voice. Led by Big Neil they were giving a loud boisterous rendition of 'Delilah', much to the amusement of the pub regulars. Neil had obviously forgotten why he was called Big Neil, as he attempted to get onto a table to lead the singing, bumping his head on the ceiling as he did so. That didn't stop him, mind, as he was soon up again and straight into the next song.

Unexpectedly the pub was then taken over by a coachload of Doncaster Rovers fans stopping off for a drink on the way back from watching a game. They were a bit perplexed as to why the pub was full of loud, drunk Welshmen. I started a conversation with one of them at the bar and on finding out that we were from the Rhondda Valley, he exclaimed, 'My mate moved down there from Doncaster a couple of years ago... you might know him? His name is Kevin Carr'. We both found ourselves laughing together when I told him that Kevin was a friend, and even a cricket team mate of mine. He was also a regular at the Con. Small world!

The night descended into a drunken blur as we took in the bright lights that Ashby had to offer. On returning to our hotel I raised my concerns about where the fire escape was. I always like to know the way out, just in case. 'There it is', Hughesy said, and pointed to a door with a fire escape sign close by.

'I'll just check it', I said, and opened the door. To my surprise – and a greater surprise to them – I saw a man and woman in bed! Either the sign was wrong or I was so drunk I opened the wrong door! Anyway, I cannot apologise enough to the couple I woke up. I went to bed thinking what a great day it had been, and hoping there wouldn't be a fire later on as I hadn't a clue where the fire escape was.

The next day, and the bus was ready to take a group of hungover Welshmen across the border for our triumphant return to Wales. The Anglo-Welsh Cup was proudly sitting on the front seat.

It was not long before the drinking games started. Can-bolters were the main competition today: a straight race to finish your can first, in an FA Cup-style knock-out tournament. Jonny Gardner and Craig Pugh made the final. But it was a bit like a one-sided FA Cup final between Man City and Rochdale, as Jonny won easily. Jonny celebrated his can-bolter crown by bolting another can in celebration.

Shortly after, Dorian the driver eventually gave in to the shouts of 'piss stop' and stopped the bus for a comfort break on the side of the motorway. We must have looked a right sight, 25 boys all lined up against the side of the bus taking a comfort break.

We were stopping for yet another comfort break further down the motorway when Hughesy suddenly got a call from the Carol, the league secretary. Concerned, she asked where we were – because the Anchor were waiting for us for our 2pm fixture.

It became immediately clear to Hughesy, and us, that he had forgotten to inform the league we were not able to play this weekend and hadn't cancelled our fixture. 'Arrrrr... Carol, we are on the M5 on the way home from our tour to Ashby.'

I could hear Hughesy drunkenly explaining: 'Tell the Anchor I don't think we will make it for kick off!' You were not wrong there, Mr Hughes. The game was void and quite correctly the three points were awarded to the Anchor. This did not detract from a tour that will live long in the memory of all of the boys who attended – and hopefully some of the Ashby boys as well.

Those memories could have been quite short-lived for skipper Gardner, as he nearly carked it on the final leg of the journey home. After polishing off another can-bolter and in mid-song, he slipped and fell down the central aisle of the bus as we descended a steep hill into Clydach Vale. Time stood still as Jonny slid down the aisle, straight towards the window at the front of the bus and, potentially, out onto the road. Luckily for Jonny (and us), co-pilot Sid's seat was in front of the window. He took a heavy blow as Jonny slid into him, arms and legs flailing everywhere.

Sid bravely exclaimed that he was not hurt despite obviously being in some pain. The event didn't seem to bother Jonny too much, as he rose to his feet to a loud roar and cheer from the rest of the bus, and promptly cracked open another can to bolt.

As we arrived back in the club, I placed the Anglo-Welsh Cup safely and proudly behind the bar. The drinking continued, with us telling tales of our tour abroad and the 5-0 victory in England to anyone we could get to listen. The cup is still fondly looked at today, and it brings back tales and memories of our tour abroad to sunny Ashby-de-la-Zouch.

Our final league game of the season saw us lose 1-0 away to Maerdy. No surprise or change there, then.

Maindy Con player awards – Season 4:

Players' Player of the Year: Jonny Gardner

Player of the Year: Lee Scott

Top Goal Scorer: Darren White

Ferndale Veterans team before our last game of last season, in front of the actual famous Dave's Coaches bus made famous in *Gavin and Stacey*

Reflections

GRASSROOTS FOOTBALL – 'real football' – has provided me with excellent times, brilliant memories and lifelong friends. I am still in love with the game today, just as I was when I made my football debut for Ton and Gelli Boys' Club under 10s team aged seven. I am still playing, despite recently turning 45, and am currently representing local club Ferndale and District in the Wales Veterans' League. Veterans' football is surprisingly competitive. It's an excellent way to prolong playing and again meet people with a similar love of the game. The Veterans' League boasts former professional players like Lee Trundle, Kris O'Leary and Damon Searle.

Veterans' football or not, when I receive the ball at my feet I feel the same instant thrill, and suddenly I am seven years old again. If I get a goal (and I got three this season!) then I can't tell you the joy.

My aim is to try to play for another two seasons, body willing, meaning that I will have played 11-a-side football for 40 consecutive seasons – the majority of them since I was advised, at the age of 19, that I would not be able to play football again. No mean feat. Doctors, eh! What do they know?

My life in local football means I can go for a drink anywhere in the Rhondda Valley and often further afield,

Four ex-Maindy Con players now playing for the Ferndale Veterans

and meet someone I have either played alongside or against. At these meetings, conversations quickly return to various games and incidents that have taken place. This gives me a feeling of great pride and a sense of being part of the football and wider community.

If you have enjoyed any of the stories in my book, remember they are not just stories to me and the boys mentioned: they are actual events, and now pleasant memories that are frequently recounted over numerous pints in the club; I imagine, and sincerely hope, this will continue to be the case in the future.

There is even some talk of organising a night to commemorate our South Wales Intermediate Cup win. (I know – any excuse for a piss-up!)

My abiding advice to you, the football fan reader, is to go out and do it yourself. Start a team, join a local league and make your own grassroots football adventures and memories. As the Premier League becomes more money-orientated and distant, you can actually get out there and live grassroots football. I can assure you that you will have some fun along the way.

You might even win something, like Maindy Con FC did. You can then reminisce about these over a pint or two in the years to come. At the same time, you'll be doing your bit for your local community by helping to keep your local pub and/or club to stay open.

To use a football phrase: if you don't shoot you don't score!

Grassroots football in the rain in Clydach Vale

The joy of Rhondda football

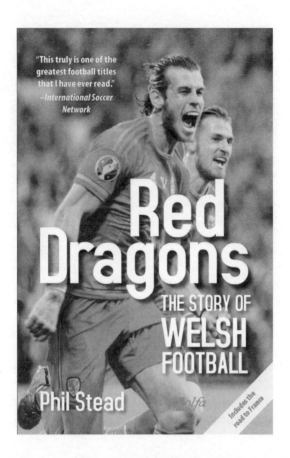

Red Dragons covers the story of Welsh football since its earliest
days in the nineteenth century, and looks at the characters,
controversies and developments of the country's clubs, players,
and most importantly, the national team – including a chapter
on the Road to France.

ISBN: 9781784612368
Price: £9.99

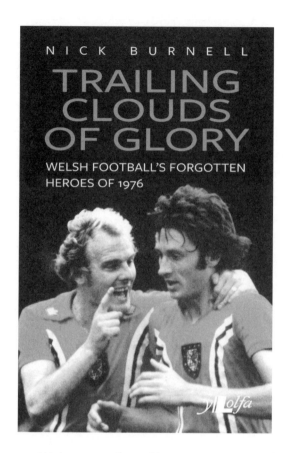

In two years, Wales went from Home International wooden spoon holders four times running to 1976 European Football Championship quarter-finalists. The book provides the background to qualification, accounts of all matches, examination of the fallout from the campaign's controversial ending, and a 'Where are they now?' section.

ISBN: 9781912631179
Price: £9.99

For a full list of our sports and other titles, go now to our website, where you may browse and buy on-line – but support your local shop if you can.

www.ylolfa.com